Demographic Trends and Economic Reality

Demographic Trends and Economic Reality

Planning and Markets in the 80's

George Sternlieb
James W. Hughes
and
Connie O. Hughes

CENTER FOR URBAN POLICY RESEARCH

Published in the United States of America
by the Center for Urban Policy Research
Building 4051—Kilmer Campus
New Brunswick, New Jersey 08903

Library of Congress Cataloging in Publication Data
Sternlieb, George.
Demographic trends and economic reality.

Includes index.
1. United States—Population—Economic aspects.
2. United States—Economic conditions—1971-
I. Hughes, James W. II. Hughes, Connie O. III. Title
HB3505.S733 1982 330.973'0927 82-12876
ISBN 0-88285-081-4

Contents

List of Exhibits

Introduction

The long-term basic shifts in America are often obscured by the transient — by the requirements to "stay in business." Immediate exigencies and fast paybacks for current decisions dominate national thinking. More profound evolutionary trends tend to be submerged in a society that has been reduced to viewing the week-to-week money-supply figures as a definitive Ouija board —with seven-day cycles of elation and/or panic resulting from trivial fluctuations. While underlying secular forces are often acknowledged, this is far more ritual than vital. The time lag in integrating them is enormously costly, as witness the debate over which neighborhood school to close, or where the water for western growth nodes is to come from — and can it get there in time to avert disaster?

Beneath the surface of momentary issues are evolutionary tides whose long-term impact promises to dwarf the more visible problem areas of the postwar era. And one of the major forces of change in this context is the web of population dynamics and its evolving form and structure. In diverse phenomena ranging from land use to diaper sales, there are no significant areas of our lives — or developmental patterns — which are not deeply associated with this reality. And certainly never more so than at present.

The sweeping changes in the demographic profile of America have certainly not escaped the attention of the popular media. Abounding are ominous stories of the tidal wave of the elderly rapidly depleting the limited store chest of social security, with the burden of support soon to be thrust upon a hard-pressed younger generation. Equivalent tales are told indicating that clearance sales should be held on educational facilities — and that a teacher's license is a passport to functional obsolescence. Yet these concerns are very real and represent but a limited sample of the far-ranging consequences of the demographic changes that are underway.

Fortunately, projections in the population domain, at least at the national scale, are far from being as obscure as is the case in many other areas. Unlike the pattern of future international relations or of technological advance — both of which are subject to the idiosyncracies of individuals and the vagaries of events that are beyond precise definition — one can forecast with considerable reliability the number of women of childbearing years over the next decade and a half (though not the number of children which they will decide to bear), the size of the working-age population for an even longer period (though not their labor-force participation patterns), and a variety of other phenomena. Consequently, while prognostication is always hazardous, there are certain demographic parameters that can be anticipated with some degree of confidence.

But at best, knowledge of the long line flywheel can be deceiving. An example is the product of the tremendous postwar surge in fertility rates which we now label the baby boom. Many marketers who accurately gauged this avalanche, and successfully "rode" its early life-cycle stages, have been bankrupted by its more mature functional vagaries — as witness the demise of the early hard-goods discounters. The effective demographics of tomorrow may not be those of yesterday; the aging baby boom has now been subjected to a profound series of segmenting forces: of household configuration, of income, of regional shift.

Equally problematic is the mutual feedback of specific demographic trends with economic forces. The interlocking relationships between demographics and the economy still defy vigorous analysis. Clearly, however, population growth within an ebullient economy fed the flame of general business vigor in the first post-World War II generation. But one of the major questions of our own time is to define the impact of the phenomenon in the midst of relative stagnation. *The demographics of affluence, from a market perspective, are very different from the results given a relatively fixed pool of wealth. And it is the latter which defines the governing circumstances of America since the 1973 energy crisis.*

The general housing demand forecasts of just a few years ago viewed the coming into the buying-power mainstream of an enormous cohort of Americans as ensuring record rates of housing production. But this expectation has suddenly aborted. The years of the American Raj have been followed by an era typified by such phrases as the "mid-life crisis of America" and the "age of the scared American."

The shortcomings of mechanistic extrapolation of history, when the economic matrix shifts, are evident. Past relationships may suddenly falter in their predictive capacity. The very formation of households is substantially shaped by housing buying power and housing availability as well as by raw demographic profiles. The years of undoubling and reduction in size of the enormously varied residential configurations, whch we lump under the term "household," were a tribute to affluence. The utilization of past household headship rates, which in turn were predicated upon an abundant supply of relatively inexpensive housing, have suddenly been brought into sharp question.

The terrifying gap between forecasts of new American automobile consumption, predicated on the historic calculus of demographics, and actual consumer behavior in the face of a massive transfer of personal-transportation-expenditure funds to energy, has become obvious. And this is to cite merely one of the many failures of projective techniques which have been enormously costly, not only to the companies involved, but indeed to the economy as a whole.

The Newtonian law that bodies set in motion tend to remain in motion unless compelled to change by external forces requires much more wariness by planners, policymakers and market researchers, given the complexity of our social/economic environment. The rise of the working wife, the role of the two-income household, the decline (or rise) of fertility rates as cause or consequence, and the folkways and marketing ways which have followed in the wake of these phenomena must be tested. Are they merely transient? Or are they shaped in a rigid matrix of economic necessity that will perpetuate them? These questions are not simple ones — we have attempted to provide some insight into their answers.

One of the quandries of public and private planners has been the rapid shift of people, jobs, and ultimately income and buying power within the United States. Certainly in the public sphere, our areal abstractions have typically been a generation behind the rush of events; the regional shifts were well underway while the focus of concern was still on individual central cities. The last year of the Carter administration saw the promulgation of the Community Conservation Guidance mandate, which provided for a federal review of suburban shopping-center development just as the boom in the latter subsided with a saturation of prime markets.

There is a fateful tendency for concept to lag behind reality, for the "expert" to reflect past textbook principles and historic experiences that may be at variance with the cutting edge of the present. Equally deleterious, however, is the tendency toward "shooting the rapids," of generalizing on momentary stress, i.e., of a brief faltering in the national economy being viewed with an apocalyptic eye.

The full measure of America's accomplishments in the decade of the 1970s has been seen through the gray filter of stagflation, of the rise of competing nations such as West Germany and Japan as the new success stories in company with some of the nations which a brief while ago were in the ranks of "the third world." Brazil and Mexico, and the newcomers of Southeast Asia, view the 1980s as the era in which their economies, income levels, and technical achievements will make them full partners in the advanced industrial world. The complacency of Americans has been shaken, the vision of a monolithic United States industrial hegemony shattered. But these challenges can be viewed not as cause for despair but rather as stimuli. The "new countries" are not merely competitors but also, increasingly, growth markets. And certainly the accomplishments of the United States in terms of assimilating the stresses of its unique demographic pattern have no parallel in Germany and Japan as indicated by some of the analyses presented within this book.

The demographics of the 1980s in and of themselves provide a much greater balance than those of the earlier decade, e.g., the phenomena of the baby boom and baby bust will be greatly attenuated. If they can be matched with a vibrant economy they will provide a base for the future social imperatives of job advancement for the maturing products of the baby boom as well as meeting the needs of the increasing cohort of the elderly. Success in this endeavor requires a full understanding of the demographic potentials for vigorous growth — and the perils of failure and frustration.

THE BROADER OBJECTIVE

In this effort we have attempted to provide a concise overview of the basic data with which to analyze the major demographic and economic trends of America as they have evolved in the recent past and as they promise to extend themselves in the short-term future. The perspective is not one of the professional demographer, but rather that of the planner, concerned with the implications of broad social and economic parameters for public and private decision making and planning. As such, future directions and their consequences are of major import.

Our working hypothesis is that the economic matrix of the 1980s will have a pronounced impact on demography to come. While select demographic parameters are assured regardless of economic change, others will be vitally affected. The latter, certainly, are subject only to reasoned speculation, and we have taken only a tentative step in this direction. But it is clear that the evolving economic shape of America will reinforce some long-standing demographic trendlines, and alter others with considerable vigor.

ORGANIZATION

Within the framework of a limited objective — a concise overview of recent demographic and economic trends —it has been necessary to strictly limit and demarcate the scope of the subject matter considered. The range and richness of the data base is such that very difficult decisions regarding inclusion and exclusion were continually faced. Our goal is to provide the primary basic building blocks of data and to suggest some of their general implications.

The analysis begins at the very general level of broad national population-growth trends and then focuses on two internal facets — age structure and household composition. Subsequently, attention is directed to the impact of these factors on the labor force, first in terms of individuals, and then as family units. The effect of the national economic environment on these elements is then presented, and connections to income patterns considered. The intersection of economic and demographic events is further evaluated in terms of consumption expenditures and the housing arena. Finally, the spatial redistribution of America's people and jobs is described both as to the evolving patterns and their linkage to the dynamics underlying the preceding demographic and economic trendlines. The detailed chapter partitions are as follows:

Chapter 1: The National Growth Deceleration

The general slowdown in national population-growth rates is analyzed in the context of fertility-rate patterns and the experience of West Germany and Japan.

Chapter 2: Age Structure Evaluation

Present, and future-age structure profiles of the United States are examined, focusing particularly on three major phenomena: the baby boom, baby bust, and growth of the elderly. General implications are suggested and an international comparison provided.

Chapter 3: Household Compositional Changes

The basic transformation of America's households is presented, targeting size and configurational attributes. Major causal elements are detailed, and probable future patterns analyzed.

Chapter 4: Population and Labor-Force Growth Patterns

The sharp divergence between general population growth and changes in the labor force, particularly the female labor force, is evaluated, linkages to household changes are suggested, comparisons to the experiences of West Germany and Japan provided, and future growth patterns detailed.

Chapter 5: Family and Employment Characteristics

The employment characteristics of husband-and-wife households have been impacted by the broader changes in America's labor-force structures. These shifts are detailed in terms of working wives and multiple-worker families.

Chapter 6: The Economic Environment

The preceding phenomena — population, household, and labor-force changes — are linked to the matrix of the economy in which they take place. This chapter presents some of the basic economic parameters which help both to define past demographics as well as to establish boundary conditions for the future.

Chapter 7: Family Income: Affluence and Stagnation

The intersection of demographic and economic events — of the working patterns of American families in a less expansive economic era — are revealed by trends in median family income. The basic realities of the immediate past are explored, and economic constraints on future demographics suggested.

Chapter 8: The Baby Boom and Consumption

The impact of income and economic constraints upon the maturing baby boom generation is analyzed in terms of consumption expenditures. The necessity for refined and defined market segmentation rather than broad demographic trend analysis is explored.

Chapter 9: Demographics and Housing

Changes in America's economic matrix, their impact on housing, and the linkages between housing and demographics are examined. The effects of changing housing parameters on the demographics of the 1980s are suggested.

Chapter 10: Changing Regional Distribution: Population

All of the demographic-economic elements of the preceding chapters are crosscut by changing patterns of regional population growth. Long-term dynamics and their recent acceleration are isolated and general ramifications noted.

Chapter 11: Changing Regional Distribution: Employment

Paralleling differential regional population growth patterns are the complementary changes in the regional distribution of jobs. Detailed employment shifts partitioned by industrial sector are analyzed in both long-and short-term time frames on regional and divisional bases.

Chapter 12: Population Distribution: Metropolitan, Nonmetropolitan, and Intrametropolitan

The resurgence of nonmetropolitan areas as population growth poles, the stabilization of metropolitan population levels, and the increasing differential between central city and suburban areas (intrametropolitan) are evaluated, and linkages to regional shifts suggested.

Appendix A: Restructured Employment Sectors

The derivation of alternative employment partitions (utilized in Chapter 6) to reflect an increasingly segmented national economy is presented, detailing all of the compositional elements.

Appendix B: International Employment Growth Patterns

Growth and change in America's employment structure is compared to that of West Germany and Japan, with similarities and divergences highlighted.

Chapter One

THE NATIONAL GROWTH DECELERATION

The issues of coping with, enjoying, and exploiting the maturing baby boom have obscured the realities of the new wave that has succeeded it. The most dominant and persisting theme of America's evolving demographic profile in the past twenty years has been the deceleration of the population-growth *rate*.[1] This is a key input into the years to come. Does it represent a resumption of a century-long trend of decline interrupted by post-World War II ebullience, or is it a momentary aberrant? What are the contours of the basic evolution?

THE OVERALL PERSPECTIVE

Exhibit 1 presents the total population estimates of the United States from 1950 to 1980 by ten-year intervals, as well as the changes for each of these periods. Over the entire 30-year time span, the population of the nation increased by more than 75 million people — more than the total population of West Germany (61 million), the equivalent of two-thirds of the total population of Japan (116 million). The manifestations of this growth are evident at every hand — from the enormous sweep of suburbia to the burgeoning restaurant industry.

But the expansion has been far from constant. As detailed at the bottom of Exhibit 1, the rate of growth has declined from the 1950 to 1960 peak of 18.5 percent to the 1970 to 1980 equivalent of 11.5 percent. The absolute increase of the 1970 to 1980 period was 4.7 million people less than that experienced from 1950 to 1960.

The pattern is highlighted as the last decade is examined in more detail.[2]

EXHIBIT 1
Resident Population of the United States:
1950 to 1980
(Numbers in Thousands)

	Population Level
Year	**Population Level**
1950	151,326
1960	179,323
1970	203,212
1980	226,505

	Population Change	
Period	**Number**	**Percent**
1950-1960	27,997	18.5
1960-1970	23,889	13.3
1970-1980	23,293	11.5

Note: Decennial census counts (April 1) not adjusted for undercounting.

Source: U.S. Bureau of the Census, Census of the Population: 1970, Vol. 1, *Characteristics of the Population,* Part 1, United States Summary -Section 1, U.S. Government Printing Office, Washington, D.C., 1973; U.S. Bureau of the Census, Current Population Reports, Series P-20, No. 363, *Population Profile of the United States: 1980,* U.S. Government Printing Office, Washington, D.C., 1981.

Exhibit 2 presents annual estimates of the population of the United States from 1970 to 1980. (It should be noted that the data of Exhibit 2 are revised estimates, taking into account errors of closure based on 1980 census results. Thus they are greater in magnitude than previously published estimates.[3]) Despite an ever-increasing base, the annual growth increment declined from 3.5 million people in 1970 to below 2.0 million in 1973. However, between 1973 and 1980, fluctuations in the annual increments have been the most noticeable pattern, raising some important issues that bear on the immediate future.

Key to the variations shown in Exhibit 2 are three factors — births, deaths, and immigration — which comprise the basic causal components of population change. The birth level is the consequence not only of the rate of fertility (the number of births that a woman would have in her lifetime, if, at each year of age, she experienced the birth rate occurring in the specified year), but also the number of women of child-bearing age, i.e., given equivalent fertility rates, a base of 1,000 women of a given age distribution will produce fewer children than a base of 1,100 women. Nonetheless, fertility is a telling indicator by itself, and deserves immediate attention.[4]

EXHIBIT 2
Preliminary Estimates of the Intercensal Population of the United States: 1970 to 1980
(Numbers in Thousands)

Population Level

Year	Population
1970 (April 1)	203,302[1]
1971 (July 1)	206,827
1972 (July 1)	209,284
1973 (July 1)	211,357
1974 (July 1)	213,342
1975 (July 1)	215,465
1976 (July 1)	217,563
1977 (July 1)	219,760
1978 (July 1)	222,095
1979 (July 1)	224,567
1980 (April 1)	226,505

Annual Increase

Period	Absolute Increase	Percent Increase
1970-1971	3,525	1.73
1971-1972	2,457	1.19
1972-1973	2,073	0.99
1973-1974	1,985	0.94
1974-1975	2,123	1.00
1975-1976	2,098	0.97
1976-1977	2,197	1.01
1977-1978	2,335	1.06
1978-1979	2,472	1.11
1979-1980	1,938	0.86

Note: [1]Adjusted to reflect undercounting.

Source: U.S. Bureau of the Census, *Current Population Reports,* Series P-25, No. 899.

FERTILITY RATES

Exhibit 3 presents one of the key touchstones of the demographers' art form, indicating the trends in fertility over the past three decades. (As a point of reference, a total fertility rate of 2.115 represents "replacement level" fertility or zero population growth, for the total populalation under current mortality conditions.) In the 1950 to 1954 period, the total rate was at the 3.337 level, i.e., 3,337 children would be born per 1,000 women. The peak in

EXHIBIT 3
Total Fertility Rate: 1950 to 1979 by Five-Year Periods and 1970 to 1980 by Year

Period	Total Fertility Rate[1]
1950-1954	3.337
1955-1959	3.690
1960-1964	3.449
1965-1969	2.622
1970-1974	2.106
1975-1979	1.807
Year	
1970	2.480
1971	2.275
1972	2.022
1973	1.896
1974	1.857
1975	1.799
1976	1.768
1977	1.826
1978	1.800
1979	1.840
1980	1.875

Note: [1]The fertility rate indicates how many births a woman would have by the end of her childbearing years if, during her entire reproductive period, she were to experience the age-specific birth rates for the given period.

Source: U.S. Bureau of the Census, Current Population Reports, Series P-20, No. 363, *Population Profile of the United States: 1980,* U.S. Government Printing Office, Washington, D.C., 1981.

modern times was experienced in the 1955 to 1959 period when it increased to 3.690. Since that time, it has decreased very sharply, with the 1975 to 1979 average fertility rate standing at 1.807, a level below the replacement threshold.

Just how precipitous this decline has been is revealed in the latter half of Exhibit 3, where the rate for each individual year of the 1970s is presented. There appears to be an inexorable and steady decline in this benchmark through 1976. Indeed, the 1.768 rate of 1976 is 29 percent less than the 2.480 rate of 1970, and almost 17 percent below the replacement level rate. Since 1976, slight upward fluctuations to the vicinity of 1.875 have been evidenced, a rate still considerably below the replacement level threshold.

This does not mean, however, that the population of the United States, even without immigration, faces imminent decline; given the increasing number of women of childbearing age, the immediate prospect is for sustained net natural increases (births minus deaths) in the nation's total population. But it does indicate that over a longer period of time, if the present fertility rate persists, the future population of the United States, sans immigration, would be reduced — and significantly. The future implications of this possibility will be returned to later; but to highlight the present situation, a summary of the detailed components of population change is necessary.

THE COMPONENTS OF POPULATION CHANGE[5]

As shown in Exhibit 4, reflecting in large part the continual decrease in the fertility rate over the 1970 to 1976 period — and the slight upward movement thereafter — the net natural increase declined from 1.8 million people in 1970 to below 1.2 million people in 1973, then proceeded to rise very slowly above 1.2 million between 1973 and 1976 and then past the 1.6 million mark by 1980. The same pattern is evident in the total number of births, with an apparent bottoming out in 1973, and a steady upward shift through 1980. As will be considered in the following chapter, these upward movements are a conse-

EXHIBIT 4

Natural Increase of the Population of the United States: 1970 to 1980[1]

(Numbers in Thousands)

Year	Natural Increase: Net	Natural Increase: Births	Natural Increase: Deaths	Net Civilian Migration[2]
1970	1,812	3,739	1,927	438
1971	1,626	3,556	1,930	387
1972	1,293	3,258	1,965	325
1973	1,163	3,137	1,974	331
1974	1,225	3,160	1,935	316
1975	1,251	3,144	1,894	449
1976	1,258	3,168	1,910	353
1977	1,426	3,327	1,900	394
1978	1,403	3,328	1,925	427
1979	1,560	3,468	1,908	460
1980	1,605	3,589	1,984	654

Note: [1]Data are for calendar years.
[2]The 1975 migration total includes the Vietnamese refugees and the 1980 total reflects the Cuban and Haitian refugees.

Source: U.S. Bureau of the Census, Current Population Reports, Series P-20, No. 363, *Population Profile of the United States: 1980,* U.S. Government Printing Office, Washington, D.C., 1981.

quence of the changing age structure of the United States. Nonetheless, the reduction in the number of births in the 1970s is emphasized by the magnitude of those recorded at the 1957 peak (4.308 million); more than 1.1 million more births occurred in 1957 than in 1975, and 700,000 more than in 1980.

At the same time, net civilian immigration, while significant, is of considerably less magnitude, generally averaging 400,000 persons per year. Unfortunately, the changing dimensions of illegal immigration into the United States are not captured by the standard data accounts. Current estimates of the absolute size of this population vary enormously, from relatively trivial numbers to above 10 million people. The net annual additions to such purported bases are even hazier in estimate. Nonetheless, this is a significant phenomenon and will be returned to in the discussion of population and the labor force (chapter 4).

AN INTERNATIONAL PERSPECTIVE

How unique to the United States are the preceding population contours? To gain insight into this question, a brief comparison to the corresponding statistics of West Germany and Japan — two other advanced industrial economies — proves useful. In terms of population growth, the United States stands intermediate between these two countries over the 1969 to 1979 period (Exhibit 5).[6] It is West Germany that exhibits the slowest overall growth (2.2 percent), gaining only 1.3 million people over 10 years. This virtual stability stands in marked contrast to the much more vigorous 13.3 percent increase registered by Japan.

Two components of change — births and net migration — amplify these differentials. Births in West Germany declined by 35.6 percent over the 1969 to 1979 period, far different from the United States and Japan. Indeed, the experience of the latter two countries provides a mirror image of one another. The number of births in the United States declined through 1974 and then proceeded to rise. In Japan, an increase was registered through 1974, with a substantial decline then evident through 1979.

In the early 1970s, the substantially higher birth rates in Japan contributed to its high rate of population growth over the decade. But by 1979, the United States, despite the substantial declines in fertility noted earlier in the chapter, had the highest crude birth rate. Indeed, the 1974 to 1979 trendline shows a sharp divergence of America with these two other economies.

The same variation is also extant in migration. The United States has had a consistently high level of inmigration while Japan generally registers outmigration. The West German context is somewhat more complex. As will be discussed in Chapter 4, labor force shortages in Germany necessitate the importation of "guest" workers during expansionary periods; but during downturns, such as 1974, outmigration ensued (Exhibit 5).

EXHIBIT 5
Comparative Population Statistics:
United States, West Germany and Japan
1969-1979
(Numbers in Thousands)

Population

	1969	1979	Change: 1969 to 1979 Number	Change: 1969 to 1979 Percent
United States	202,677	220,584	17,907	8.8%
West Germany	60,067	61,359	1,292	2.2
Japan	102,320	115,880	13,560	13.3

Births (Absolute Number)

	1969	1974	1979
United States	3,630	3,160	3,468
West Germany	903	626	582
Japan	1,907	2,046	1,654

Crude Birth Rates[1]

	1969	1974	1979
United States	17.9	14.9	15.9
West Germany	16.1	10.1	9.5
Japan	18.7	18.6	14.3

Net Migration

	1969	1974	1979
United States	453	316	460
West Germany	572	-9	246
Japan	10	-20	-12

Note: [1]Births per 1000 population.

Source: OECD (Organization for Economic Cooperation and Development), *Labor Force Statistics: 1969-1979,* Paris, 1981.

Thus the United States population-growth deceleration is not unique in the context of advanced industrial economies. Even at the beginning of the 1980s, its birth rate still stood much higher than its two economic peers.

THE FUTURE

Given the pattern of steadily decreasing rates of population increase over the past thirty years and the "plateauing" of the rate of fertility in the last decade, what are the short-term expectations for national population growth?[7] Variations in the future will continue to be a function of the fertility rate and the number of women of child-bearing age, assuming that mortality rates and immigration levels do not change significantly.

As will be explored subsequently, the number of women of child-bearing age in the United States will be increasing significantly over the 1980s — the products of the maturation of the post-World War II baby boom — making it possible for the number of births to increase even in the context of reduced fertility. Additionally, the sheer size of the fertile cohorts could amplify any positive fertility-rate fluctuations into much larger population-growth consequences.

The Census Bureau's most recent projection sets comprise three different series, each reflecting different assumptions about the rate of fertility.[8] These rates are assumed to move toward the following levels:

Series I - 2.7
Series II - 2.1
Series III - 1.7

Additionally, all assume a slight improvement in mortality and an annual net immigration of 400,000 people. Exhibit 6 presents the 1990 and 2000 projections, with the 1980 to 1990 growth anticipated between 9.3 million and 27.7 million people. The upper bound is probably unrealistic in light of the fertility-rate experience of the immediate past. The most likely expectation is an increase similar to the Series II projection — 17 million — somewhat below the experience of the 1970s.

The effects of differential fertility rates will tend to pyramid as the span of time lengthens. Hence from 1990 to 2000, the range of absolute increase broadens to between 7.6 million and 28.1 million people. If the fertility rate experiences a sharp upsurge — a probability that will be subsequently entertained — the total United States population will approach the 283-million-person level by the year 2000; if the present rate is maintained, the population projection would approach 250 million. While the implications of these alternative paths are significant — for example, influencing desired housing formats in the immediate future, and the nation's educational infrastructure in a slightly longer range framework — America's future economic and social life will still be dominated by the extant population. This situation should be evident as we examine the internal composition of the nation's populace — the age structure evolution.

SUMMARY

The issue of controlling and managing growth gained the center stage of the planning profession in the decade of the 1970s. Following two decades of growth aspirations, the nation's suburbs, in concert with broader national

EXHIBIT 6

Decade Census and Projected Population of the United States: 1980, 1990, 2000

(Numbers in Thousands)

			Change 1980-1990			Change 1990-2000	
	1980*	**1990****	**Number**	**Percent**	**2000****	**Number**	**Percent**
Population	227,002	I. 254,715	27,713	12.2	282,837	28,122	11.0
		II. 243,513	16,511	7.3	260,378	16,865	6.9
		III. 236,264	9,262	4.1	243,876	7,612	3.2

Notes: *As of April 1, 1980 from 1980 Census counts.

**As of July 1 of respective years.

1. Includes Armed Forces overseas.

2. The projections were prepared using the "cohort-component" method and comprise three Series — I, II, and III. All assume a slight improvement in mortality, an annual net immigration of 400,000, and completed cohort fertility rates (i.e., average number of lifetime births per 1,000 women) that move toward the following levels: Series I — 2,700; Series II —2,100; Series III — 1,700.

Source: U.S. Bureau of the Census, Current Population Reports, Series P-20, No. 363, *Population Profile of the United States: 1980,* U.S. Government Printing Office, Washington, D.C., 1981.

U.S. Bureau of the Census, Current Population Reports, Series P-25, No. 704, *Projections of the Population of the United States: 1975 to 2050,* U.S. Government Printing Office, Washington, D.C., July 1977.

movements, increasingly began to entertain the wisdom of no-growth. And this at a time when the gross population gain had already faltered. Belated theory began to belabor a trend which had already peaked.

1. For each successive ten-year interval over the past thirty-year period (1950 to 1980), both the absolute population-growth increment of the United States and the rate of increase declined significantly.
2. From 1950 to 1960, the nation's population increased by 28 million people (18.5 percent). The equivalent growth for the 1970 to 1980 period was 23 million (11.5 percent).
3. For 1970-1971, the annual total growth was 3.5 million people (1.73 percent). By 1979-1980, the annual increment declined to 1.9 million people (0.86 percent). The nation's total resident population as of April 1, 1980, was estimated at 226.5 million people, compared to 203 million people in 1970.
4. Underlying this pervasive slowdown was the decline in the fertility rate, which reached its nadir in 1976 at 1.768, By 1980, the rate gradually shifted upward to 1.875 but still far below the replacement level of 2.115.
5. The fertility rate is the most critical assumption determining future population estimates. The Census Bureau's Series III projection, which employs a fertility rate somewhat above present reality, indicates that the total population of the United States in 1990 will approach 245 million, implying a growth increment somewhat smaller than the recent past, despite the sharp increases in the number of women of child-bearing age who will have started to push growth upward in the 1980s.

Chapter Two

AGE STRUCTURE EVOLUTION

There are three major phenomena that have shaped the last thirty years and whose implications will be basic to the future: the baby boom, the baby bust, and the growth of the elderly population. While precise delineations vary, the post-World War II baby boom was initiated in 1946 by an approximately 20-percent increase in the number of live births compared to that recorded in 1945. A steady increase in the annual number of births continued to 1957, the peak year of the post-war era. About 47 million children were born over a 12-year span, accounting for about 21 percent of the 1980 population. It is this group which has inserted a permanent but moving bulge into America's age structure, flooding the nation's school systems in the 1950s and 1960s, its higher educational system in the 1960s and 1970s, and its job and housing markets in the 1970s and 1980s.

The subsequent baby bust, by definition, is already being felt as it trails in the wake of the baby boom. While the latter produced 47 million children during the 12-year period from 1946 to 1957, the equivalent in the 12-year period from 1965 to 1976 was only 41 million. Facilities and opportunities predicated on a larger predecessor population are now beginning to experience the initial stages of weak demand, a phenomenon that will be increasingly prevalent over this decade.

Finally, the elderly — those 65 years of age and over — are continually increasing in size and significance. Their number has more than doubled to 26 million people over the last thirty years, and now account for over 11 percent of the nation's population total (as compared to 8.1 percent in 1950).

These phenomena dominate the age-structure shifts that have taken place in the United States from 1950 to 1980, and will continue to do so in the future. In the following analysis, these changes will be evaluated decade by decade;

attempts will be made to draw correlations to recent social and economic events, and the implications for the short-term future.

THE 1950 TO 1960 PERIOD

The era of the baby boom is shown very clearly in the 1950 to 1960 data portrayed in Exhibit 7. In that decade, the population of the United States increased by 28 million people; of this increase, over 15 million were 14 years of age or under, accounting for 54 percent of the total growth. It is this bulge which already has been, and will be, basic to developmental patterns in the United States as a whole. Much of the shift to suburbia, and with it the attendant stress on educational plant development (as well as its complement, school financing problems) was a consequence of this incredible quanta.

But at the same time, a relatively low level of growth was experienced in the ranks of those 15 to 24 years of age, and an actual decline of 1.1 million people (reflecting the after-effects of reduced depression-era birth rates) between the ages of 25 to 34 years was realized. Given an expanding economy, these were years of great employment opportunities for the latter group, not the least among them the tending of the enormous increment of school-age children.

At the other end of the age spectrum was the considerable growth in the elderly population (4.3 million people); in excess of 15 percent of the total national growth increment in the decade was 65 years of age and over. This once again provided impetus for the growth of a service- and welfare-related orientation and job base for American society. However, the sheer weight of youth more than offset the elderly expansion; this is reflected in the decline of the overall median age from 30.2 years to 29.5 years, gauging the beginning of the youth orientation which was to reach full force the ensuing decade.

THE DECADE OF THE 1960'S

The 1960s marked both the entrance of the early products of the baby boom into their college age years and the advent of the baby bust. Gauging the latter was the abrupt decline (-3.2 million) from 1960 to 1970 in the level of population under the age of five. This reflected in turn the relative stagnancy in the proportion of the population in the prime child-bearing ages of 25 to 34 years during the decade, as well as a declining fertility rate.

At the same time, the 5-to-14-years-of-age sector, the last remnants of the baby boom, continued to grow but at a diminished level from the 1950s, expanding by 5.3 million people. By 1970, this cohort accounted for over 20 percent of the nation's population — 41 million people — a level almost 17 million greater than that of 1950. America's school systems were severely stressed as their clientele peaked in number.

The largest variation, however, was in the 15-to-24 years-of-age sector; in the 1950s, this cohort was virtually stable in size. In contrast, it expanded by

EXHIBIT 7

Age Structures of the Resident Population of the United States
1950-1980
(Numbers in Thousands)

Age	1950	Change 1950-1960	1960	Change 1960-1970	1970	Change 1970-1980	1980
Total	151,326	27,997	179,323	23,912	203,235	23,270	226,505
Under 5	16,243	4,078	20,321	-3,158	17,163	-819	16,344
5-14	24,430	11,035	35,465	5,308	40,773	-5,835	34,938
15-24	22,221	1,799	24,020	11,447	35,467	7,007	42,474
25-34	23,878	-1,060	22,818	2,105	24,923	12,153	37,076
35-44	21,535	2,546	24,081	-980	23,101	2,530	25,631
45-54	17,397	3,088	20,485	2,750	23,235	-438	22,797
55-64	13,327	2,245	15,572	3,030	18,602	3,098	21,700
65 and over	12,295	4,265	16,560	3,412	19,972	5,572	25,544
Median Age	30.2		29.5		28.0		30.0

Source: U.S. Bureau of the Census, Census of the Population: 1970, Vol. 1, *Characteristics of the Population,* Part 1; United States Summary - Section 1, U.S. Government Printing Office, Washington, D.C., 1973; and U.S. Bureau of the Census, Current Population Reports, Series P-20, No. 363, *Population Profile of the United States: 1980,* U.S. Government Printing Office, Washington, D.C., 1981.

11.4 million people from 1960 to 1970, and with it the rapid expansion of the nation's educational infrastructure was transferred to the college and university scene. Concurrently, however, the problems of youth unemployment —and its sad corollary of juvenile delinquency — were clearly amplified.

The elderly continued to expand in absolute number, gaining 3.4 million people. The Sun Valleys and the retirement communities of Florida and New Jersey were bolstered by vigorous growth in their prime market targets. Nonetheless, the median age of Americans dropped to 28.0 years, as the "youth society" reached its apogee.

THE 1970 TO 1980 TRANSFORMATION

The contours of the baby bust continued to eat deeper into the fabric of American society in the decade of the 1970s. The maturing products of the baby boom dominated the total growth increment — over one-half (12.2 million people) of the nation's 1970 to 1980 total growth (23.3 million people) were between the ages of 25 to 34 years, the period of household formation and peak child-bearing. Similarly, the 15-to-24-years-of-age cohort also continued to expand (7.0 million people) but at a lesser rate compared to the previous 10 years.

Despite the burgeoning of these fertile sectors of society, the declining birth rates resulted in the continued contraction in the under-5-years-of-age population (-819,000). The decline of the latter during the preceding decade now impacted the 5-to-14-years-of-age sector, which receded by 5.8 million people from 1970 to 1980. Excess capacity began to appear in the nation's school systems for the first time in the post-World War II era.

The accession rate to the ranks of the elderly expanded markedly, and because of the declining number of births, the elderly comprised almost 24 percent of the national growth increment. As a result, the median age of Americans began to creep upward (30.0 years), as the era of an aging society began.

So by 1980 the demographic outlines of the short-term future started to come into focus. The baby boom offspring are in their child-bearing years, have and are forming households and are exerting pressures on the American economy to produce not only new jobs for young adults, but also upper-level positions for their more mature peers. Similarly, the housing industry finds its major growth target a population in its thirties. To what type of housing does this group aspire? And what can they afford? These are questions of major import not only for the planning profession, but for America's political leadership as well. Subsequent chapters will explore these critical questions in the context of the nation's broader economic and housing parameters.

Contraction also is a phenomenon that is and will be increasingly felt. After three decades of struggling to cope with growth, often with indifferent results, the wake of the baby boom is characterized by shrinking age cohorts. This in turn raises the problems of redundant infrastructures, excess capacities, and declining economic sectors. The educational area provides a prime case in point as the school budget and school bond issues of yesteryear give way to the school closing issues of today.

A myriad of other concerns are raised by this age structure matrix. It is important, therefore, to examine future projections under alternative assumptions.

THE FUTURE: THE DECADE OF THE 1980'S

The decline in the birth rate through 1975 was so precipitous as to leave demographers, both inside and out of the Census Bureau, gasping in its wake. Projection has followed projection, each one lower than its predecessor, yet still overly optimistic in terms of the realities of births which followed it. Indeed, the alternative projection sets presented in the preceding chapter were issued in July 1977 and superceded those published barely 20 months previous. And since that time, updated projections have not been published. Thus the Census projections that are available and used in this book do not reflect the 1980 census counts, nor do they reflect any changed fertility-rate assumptions which may have emanated from the experience of the late 1970s. Nonetheless, one can be reasonably confident that the projections presented here provide the outlines of phenomena to come, although their precise scale may be subject to a higher degree of uncertainty.

In Exhibit 8, the results only of the Series II projection — which assumes a long-term fertility rate approaching 2.1 — are presented. It should be pointed out that for 1990 and 2000 the projections for the older groups (above 10 years in 1990 and above 20 years in 2000) are independent of the birth rate — the individuals are already alive and the total numbers of their respective age cohorts are reasonably assured, at least to the degree that mortality-rate, immigration, and baseline assumptions are valid.

The maturing products of the baby boom continue to dominate the age-structure changes — the bulk of the bulge will have aged to between 35 and 44 years of age by 1990. Indeed, the 11-million person increase in this cohort will account for over 60 percent of the national growth increment between 1980 and 1990. This will undoubtedly place enormous stress on the nation's economic system to satisfy the mid-level career aspirations of this fabled generation. Ever greater pressures for entrance into the executive suite will continue, a phenomenon only partially alleviated by a decline in the 55 to 64 years of age group.

In contrast to the expansion represented by maturing baby boomers will be the sharp contraction of the 15-to-24-years-of-age segment by approximately 7.7 million people; the baby bust, then, will finally be impacting American society in full force. Who will inherit - and support - the infrastructure built for

EXHIBIT 8

Decade Census and Projected Age Structure of the Population of the United States: 1980, 1990, 2000

(Numbers in Thousands)

Age	1980*	Change 1980 to 1990 Series II	1990** Series II	Change 1990 to 2000 Series II	2000** Series II
Total	226,505	17,008	243,513	16,865	260,378
Under 5	16,344	3,093	19,437	-1,585	17,852
5-14	34,938	820	35,758	3,395	39,153
15-24	42,474	-7,744	34,730	1,895	36,625
25-34	37,076	4,010	41,086	-6,636	34,450
35-44	25,631	10,961	36,592	4,752	41,344
45-54	22,797	2,514	25,311	10,564	35,875
55-64	21,700	-924	20,776	2,481	23,257
65 and over	25,544	4,280	29,824	1,998	31,822
Median Age	30.0		32.8		35.5

Notes: *As of April 1, 1980 from 1980 Census counts.
**As of July 1 of respective years.

Sources: U.S. Bureau of the Census, Current Population Reports, Series P-20, No. 363, *Population Profile of the United States: 1980,* U.S. Government Printing Office, Washington, D.C., 1981; and U.S. Bureau of the Census, Current Population Reports, Series P-25, No. 704, *Projections of the Population of the United States: 1977 to 2050,* U.S. Government Printing Office, Washington, D.C., 1977.

the baby-boom generation? Between 1980 and 1990, it is entirely possible that the college-age population will decline by over 18 percent, fostering significant adjustments for higher-education institutions and services. At the same time, the numbers of new entrants to the labor force will shrink over the decade (ignoring labor-force-participation rates), alleviating the entry-level job pressures that characterized the 1970s. The entry-level housing built for a larger generation may provide a redundancy of certain forms of shelter as the decade evolves.

Concurrently, with the stabilization in size of the 5-to-14-years-of-age sector — which will remain at the 35-million-person level throughout the decade of the 1980s — the nation's elementary and high schools will face diminished downward demographic pressure (although spatial population shifts will exert differential effects on a geographic base). In the aggregate, the three-decade-long stress of a boom-bust cycle should be greatly alleviated.

Once again, the elderly are a significant growth sector with a net increase of 4.3 million people expected — or roughly 450,000 persons a year reaching the nominal retirement age and surviving between 1980 and 1990. And the under-5-years-of-age population will begin to grow in size. Thus a baby-boom "echo" will become etched into the nation's age structure. But this will not preserve the United States population as a whole from a decided increase in median age to above 32 years.

When we contrast the age-structure profile of America's population in 1990 versus that of 1980, the scale of thc transformation becomes evident. There will be a growth of 4.3 million people over the age of 65. The issues of retirement, pensions, social security, and social services to the elderly will become increasingly prominent, and will place added dependency pressures on a basic economic system facing increasing international competition.

These questions may be accentuated by the decline (924,000) in the 55-to-64-years-of-age sector (the depression-era progeny), many of whom are in their peak earning years. Undoubtedly, much of the immediate burden may rest on the 35-to-44-years-of-age-group (the baby-boom products), whose number will increase by 11 million people. It is paradoxical for a group born in perhaps the most affluent period in America's history that, after facing a stagnant economy in the early 1970s and continual competition in the marketplace by virtue of their sheer numbers, their destiny is to fall heir to the responsibility and burdens of maintaining an aging society.

In contrast, the 15-to-24-years-of-age group will be in substantial decline as the major segments of the baby bust reach adulthood (-7.7 million). To say that these declines will challenge the conventions and assumptions established throughout the decade of the 1970s is to state the obvious. For example, this age group is the lifeblood of the soft-drink industry, with each individual consuming an average 823 cans of soda each year.[9] Assuming this standard is valid for the entire decade, 6.3 billion cans of soft drinks will *not* be sold in 1990 because of declines in this age group. Few industries and institutions will escape the impact of this demographic shift.

Indeed, consumption patterns will change markedly across the board. As discussed more fully in chapter 8, many retailing successes of the past decade were predicated upon the baby-boom cohort. As their expenditure patterns mature, the vacuum left in their wake will necessitate major adjustments by previously successful enterprises in order for them to survive. This will be particularly the case in a low-growth economic context (see chapters 6 and 7).

THE 1990'S

The 1990s may well be a much less "volatile" demographic decade as compared to its immediate predecessors. The massive baby-boom generation will be continually maturing into established middle-age status (40 to 50 years of age), while the growth of the elderly (2 million persons) will abate markedly (Exhibit 8). Conceivably, labor-force shortages could accompany the baby-bust generation as it moves into the 25 to 34 years of age bracket (-6.6 million persons), and as the 15-to-24-years-of-age group expands only minimally (1.9 million). The baby boom "echo" will be evidenced by a 3.4 million increase in the 5-to-14-years-of-age sector — an increment of far less magnitude than its progenitor — while a baby-bust "echo" will appear in the under 5-years-of-age population (-1.6 million). But the key demographic description of the decade may well be "maturation," as the median age of the United States population rises above 35 years.

AN INTERNATIONAL COMPARISON

At the risk of an abrupt time shift, it is useful to again place in broader context the American demographic events of the past decade. In Exhibit 9, the broad age-structure shifts in the United States over the 1969 to 1979 period are compared to their equivalents in West Germany and Japan.[10] While the United States stands intermediate in overall growth rates, it experienced far greater expansion among those in the 15 to 64 years of age. West Germany, in contrast, secured a gain of only 2.1 million persons (5.4 percent) in this age bracket, the United States equivalent was more than ten times as great (21 million). While Japan experienced substantial growth in the same age group (7.3 million persons), it lagged behind the United States significantly in rate — 10.3 percent versus 16.3 percent. Thus the pressure for sustained job expansion over the 1970s was far more severe in the United States — at least as gauged by population growth alone — and least significant in West Germany.

Nonetheless, the latter had a much more significant elderly population (15.5 percent of total population) while Japan's was growing at the fastest rate (44.9 percent). Clearly the issues attendant to large elderly populations are not unique to the United States, but are a basic reality in other advanced industrial nations. America has been unique, however, in the vast growth of its working-age population, and the concomitant stresses of job provision (see chapter 6).

EXHIBIT 9
Comparative Age Structure Shifts:
United States, West Germany and Japan
1969-1979
(Numbers in Thousands)

	1969		1979		Change: 1969-1979	
	Number	**Percent**	**Number**	**Percent**	**Number**	**Percent**
United States	202,677	100.0%	220,584	100.0%	17,907	8.8%
Under 15 years	58,260	28.7	50,213	22.8	-8,047	-13.8
15 to 64 years	124,737	61.5	145,713	66.1	20,976	16.8
65 years and over	19,680	9.7	24,658	11.2	4,978	25.3
West Germany	60,067	100.0%	61,359	100.0%	1,292	2.2%
Under 15 years	14,012	23.3	11,572	18.9	-2,440	-17.4
15 to 64 years	38,219	63.6	40,287	65.7	2,068	5.4
65 years and over	7,837	13.0	9,499	15.5	1,662	21.2
Japan	102,320	100.0%	115,880	100.0%	13,560	13.3%
Under 15 years	24,550	24.0	27,680	23.9	3,130	12.7
15 to 64 years	70,700	69.1	77,970	67.3	7,270	10.3
65 years and over	7,060	6.9	10,230	8.8	3,170	44.9

Source: OECD (Organization for Economic Cooperation and Development), *Labor Force Statistics: 1969-1979,* Paris, 1981.

SUMMARY

The shifting patterns of child bearing in the three decades following World War II have had profound impact on the age structure fabric of American society and threaten to unravel a number of instrumentalities painfully accommodated in the past.

1. The youth society is gradually fading into the history text. Significant and sustained declines in the numbers of American citizenry between the ages of 5 and 14 characterized the 1970s, a phenomenon that will shift to the 15-to-24-years-of-age sector in the 1980s.
2. Between 1970 and 1980 elementary-school enrollment in the United States declined by over 6 million pupils. Over the next decade, the balance of the nation's educational institutions will partake of the same basic trend.

3. The ranks of the elderly are expanding. In 1980, over 11.2 percent of the population of America was 65 years of age and over and will slowly increase in the future.
4. As a consequence, the nation's median age has started to increase — we are now experiencing the initial stages of what appears to be a long-term trend. The aged-dependency ratio (the population over 65 years of age per 100 population aged 18 to 64) is climbing upward. At the same time the child-dependency ratio (under 18 years of age) has declined sharply.
5. If we are in the initial stages of an aging society, does this imply the advent of a more conservative milieu? Will there be greater resistance to change and new ideas? Will the no-growth and development-resisting forces dominate the day-to-day activities of the political process (at least in the territories of affluence)?
6. The dominant age-growth sector of present and future history will be the maturing cohorts of the baby boom. The population between the ages of 25 and 44 will be expanding markedly during the 1980s and will represent significant market targets. Yet, as a consequence of demography, the progeny of the 1946 to 1957 era will find competition, particularly in the job market, their staple throughout life.
7. The present labor surplus — the mass entrance of the baby-boom product into the labor force — may well be transformed into a labor shortage over the decade of the 1980s as the shrinking cohorts of the subsequent baby bust reach adulthood. Will this result in improved job opportunities for minorities? Or will jobs be exported to foreign nations? Or, conversely, will illegal immigration continue and expand, perhaps reclassified by modification of the nation's immigration statutes? And if it is the latter set of occurrences, how will this in turn, alter the age-structure evolution?
8. Housing-market shifts at best are always difficult to predict, and even more so on the basis of population alone. Indeed, the following sections isolate patterns of household and employment trends and geographical movements which must be incorporated into any demand-and-supply equation. Still, the baby-boom dynamic promises to dictate the demand for housing in the short-term future and, ignoring other factors, will exert pressure for single-family suburban-type units.
9. A symptom of this demand was the multi-family construction surge throughout urban and suburban areas in the early 1970s. This can be construed, at least in part, as a lag effect of the baby boom. As the instigators of this demand aged, the late 1970s single-family boom resulted. Yet household-composition changes lend question to the longevity of this phenomenon. While the housing question is linked to demographics in chapter 8, household shifts must first be examined.

Chapter Three

HOUSEHOLD COMPOSITIONAL CHANGES

Absolute population totals, even when disaggregated into detailed age cohorts, sketch only a partial picture of a very complex phenomenon. Of equal importance is the way individuals cluster into household configurations — groups of persons occupying individual housing units. It is household formation that is the crucial dynamic in many markets. Interpreted in this format, the implications of population change for the housing market, for example, become much more apparent. Indeed, housing demand is not so much a function of total population size, but rather of the total number of households. At the same time, however, the reality should not be slighted that the very availability of housing in turn may alter the scale and number of households (see chapter 9). In any case, whether defining future land-use requirements or furniture sales, the realities of gross demographic variation must be viewed, at least in part, within the dynamics of household configurations. What are the realities and basic trends of this domain?

THE BROADER OUTLINES

In the period of one generation as covered by Exhibit 10, there has been a precipitous decline in the average household size in the United States. In the thirty years from 1950 to 1980, the average number of persons per household has moved from 3.37 to 2.75, a decline of 18.4 percent with an acceleration of this trend evident in the last decade.[11] The implications of this shift can be simply illustrated. Assume a political jurisdiction in 1950 having a base population of 1,000 people. By definition, if its average household size is 3.37, its occupied housing units total 297. If by 1980 its absolute population size remains at the 1,000 level, 364 housing units are implied by an average

EXHIBIT 10
Household-Size Shifts: 1950 to 1980
(Persons Per Household)

Year	Size
1950	3.37
1955	3.33
1960	3.33
1965	3.29
1970	3.14
1971	3.11
1972	3.06
1973	3.01
1974	2.97
1975	2.94
1976	2.89
1977	2.86
1978	2.81
1979	2.78
1980	2.75

Sources: U.S Bureau of the Census, *Statistical Abstract of the United States: 1980* (101st edition), Washington, D.C., 1980; and U.S. Bureau of the Census, Current Population Reports, Series P-20, No. 363, *Population Profile of the United States: 1980,* U.S. Government Printing Office, Washington, D.C., 1981.

household size of 2.75. Consequently, at the most basic level, areas of no-growth and stagnation may still experience surges of housing demand if the present household-size evolution persists into the future. Nearly half of the total increase in occupied housing in the 1970s was a reflection of decreased household size.

The transformation to date is a composite of many elements and, as holds true for all of the concerns stressed here, the push-pull factors at work are of extreme complexity. Housing availability, income realities, welfare stipulations, and the enormous number of dynamics that are causally referred to as "changing societal and cultural norms" are all of significance. The analysis in this brief work must, of necessity, be limited to a very few of the principal parameters. It should be noted, however, that these are merely the external manifestations of enormously complex phenomena. The presentation, at best, must be limited to the topography rather than the total dimensions of the realities embodied in the data.

A major tribute of the shrinking household-size reality is the changing number of children born to individual women. This is reflected in Exhibit 11, which details the total children that were born per 1,000 married women, and the percent childless for women ever married, for each of the five-year benchmarks between 1960 and 1980. Their import is very clear: for all the age groups between the ages of 24 and 45, there is a substantial decrease to the present time. (Those above 45 years of age in 1980 were the principal generators of the baby boom detailed in the previous section.) Unless there is an unparalleled increase of women having children in their later years, the future portends a continuation of the shrinking household-size trend.

As shown in the latter part of Exhibit 11, part of the pattern of decline has been the result of the growing proportion of women under the age of 30 who are married and have had no children. Again, this is a phenomenon mainly of the women entering the child-bearing years in the wake of the baby boom. But the significant question concerns the extrapolation of these recent events into

EXHIBIT 11

Children Ever Born Per 1,000 Married Women and Percent Childless for Women Ever Married 1960 to 1980

Age (in years) of Women Ever Married	Children Ever Born Per 1,000 Married Women				
	1960*	**1965****	**1970***	**1975****	**1980****
15 to 44	2,314	2,477	2,360	2,140	1,965
15 to 19	792	685	636	601	627
20 to 24	1,441	1,328	1,071	886	930
25 to 29	2,241	2,360	1,984	1,580	1,397
30 to 34	2,627	2,950	2,806	2,387	1,970
35 to 39	2,686	3,016	3,170	2,994	2,572
40 to 44	2,564	2,856	3,097	3,282	3,105
45 to 49	2,402	2,603	2,854	3,152	3,185

Age (in years) of Women Ever Married	Percent Childless for Women Ever Married				
	1960*	**1965****	**1970***	**1975****	**1980****
15 to 44	15.0	14.2	16.4	18.0	18.8
15 to 19	43.6	48.0	50.9	50.6	46.6
20 to 24	24.2	28.0	35.7	42.3	40.4
25 to 29	12.6	11.7	15.8	21.1	25.3
30 to 34	10.4	7.2	8.3	8.8	13.7
35 to 39	11.1	8.7	7.3	5.3	8.0
40 to 44	14.1	11.0	8.6	7.0	6.6
45 to 49	18.1	13.9	10.6	7.3	7.7

Notes: *As of April of respective years.
**As of June of respective years.

Source: U.S. Bureau of the Census, *Statistical Abstract of the United States: 1980* (101st edition), Washington, D.C., 1980.

the future. Grappling with this crucial issue will be reserved for the end of this section; the events to date require further elaboration and analysis.

Changing household size is not solely a function of the rise and fall of the production of children; it is also accounted for by equivalent changes in the basic marriage relationship. As shown in Exhibit 12, the two major barometers, divorce and marriage rates, show changes that imply a decline in household size. Divorce rates over the last 20 years, from 1960 to 1980, have increased by 141 percent, moving from 2.2 divorces per 1,000 population to the 5.3 level. The marriage rate has exhibited less drastic swings, but during the 1970s fluctuated between 10 and 11 marriages per 1,000 population. Nonetheless, there is some indication that the gap between the two indicators is closing. In 1950, the divorce rate was 23.4 percent of the marriage rate; by 1980, this relationship increased to 48.6 percent. While not every divorce necessarily ends in two separate households — with remarriage and other alternative living arrangements possible — it is a significant force in generating additional households.

Thus the broader outlines of a metamorphosis of the American household are apparent. A long-term decline in household size is manifest, resulting not only from declining fertility and fewer children, but from an increasing

EXHIBIT 12

Marriage and Divorce Rates: 1950-1980

Year	Marriage Rate[1]	Divorce Rate[2]
1950	11.1	2.6
1955	9.3	2.3
1960	8.5	2.2
1965	9.3	2.5
1970	10.6	3.5
1971	10.6	3.7
1972	11.0	4.1
1973	10.9	4.4
1974	10.5	4.6
1975	10.1	4.9
1976	10.0	5.0
1977	10.1	5.0
1978	10.5	5.2
1979	10.6	5.4
1980 (P)	10.9	5.3

Notes: [1]Number of marriages per 1,000 population.
[2]Number of divorces per 1,000 population.

Source: U.S. National Center for Health Statistics, *Vital Statistics of the United States*, annual.

divorce rate and a constant marriage rate. Yet household size per se provides only a surface glimpse of a very complex evolution. What are the emerging household formats?

EMERGING HOUSEHOLD FORMATS

Exhibit 13 details the composition of America's households for 1960, 1970, 1975, and 1980. While the population growth from 1960 to 1970 was 13.3 percent (Exhibit 1), the growth in households was 20.1 percent. In the 1970 to 1980 period, the former expanded by 11.5 percent while the latter increased by 24.8 percent. Hence the gap between the two rates of growth has widened — and substantially.

The most salient phenomenon in the changing format of households is the decline in importance of married-couple (husband-wife) families. In 1960, they accounted for 74.3 percent of the nation's households. By 1980, their share had declined to 60.9 percent. At the same time, female-headed families (other family, female householder) increased from 8.4 percent of the total in 1960 to 10.8 percent in 1980. Overall, family households (two or more related individuals sharing a dwelling unit), while not about to become extinct in America, have declined from 85.0 percent of the total households to 73.9 percent over this period of time.

Nonfamily households — either persons living alone or with nonrelatives only — increased quite rapidly and presently (1980) account for 26.1 percent of all households, as compared to 15.0 percent in 1960. Indeed such nonfamily households increased more than five times as fast as family households from 1970 to 1980 (73.1 percent versus 13.5 percent). This has resulted from a substantial increase in single-person households (householder living alone) — totaling 17.8 million in 1980 — as well as from the emergence of a relatively new phenomenon, nonfamily households comprising 2 or more persons. In the ten years from 1970 to 1980, this household type had the fastest growth rate of those shown here, increasing by 162 percent.

If we focus on the percentage change for the latter period, the sharpness of the current trend — partially obscured by the longer time span — becomes evident. The number of nonfamily households from 1970 to 1980 increased by 73.1 percent while other families with female householders (no husband present) increased by 55.3 percent. Even male-householder families (no wife present) increased by 38.9 percent. At the same time, however, the classic married-couple families expanded by only 7.7 percent. Consequently, what were once unique or atypical households are dominating the recent growth increment and require further analysis.

TWO-PERSON NONFAMILY HOUSEHOLDS

A significant portion of nonfamily households with non-relatives present comprise two-person formats (2.3 million out of 2.9 million such households

EXHIBIT 13
Households by Type and Size: 1960 to 1980
(Numbers in Thousands)

Households	1960		1970		1975		1980		Percent Change		
	Number	Percent	Number	Percent	Number	Percent	Number	Percent	1960-1970	1970-1975	1970-1980
TOTAL	52,799	100.0	63,401	100.0	71,120	100.0	79,108	100.0	20.1	12.2	24.8
Family Households	44,905	85.0	51,456	81.2	55,563	78.1	58,426	73.9	14.6	8.0	13.5
Married-Couple Family	39,254	74.3	44,728	70.5	46,951	66.0	48,180	60.9	13.9	5.0	7.7
Other Family, male householder	1,228	2.3	1,228	1.9	1,485	2.1	1,706	2.2	0.0	20.9	38.9
Other Family, female householder	4,422	8.4	5,500	8.7	7,127	10.0	8,540	10.8	24.4	29.6	55.3
Non-family Households	7,895	15.0	11,945	18.8	15,557	21.9	20,682	26.1	51.3	30.2	73.1
Householder Living Alone	6,896	13.1	10,851	17.1	13,939	19.6	17,816	22.5	57.4	28.5	64.2
Households of 2 or More Persons	999	1.9	1,094	1.7	1,618	2.3	2,866	3.6	9.5	47.9	162.0
Average Size of Household	3.33		3.14		2.94		2.75				

Note: Non-institutional population.

Source: U.S. Bureau of the Census, Current Population Reports, Series P-20, No. 363, *Population Profile of the United States: 1980,* U.S. Government Printing Office, Washington, D.C., 1981.

in 1980). Exhibit 14 details their configuration by age of householder (primary individual) for 1970 and 1980. Within this group, the major gains were secured by childless unmarried couples — individuals who share their living quarters with an unrelated person of the opposite sex. Indeed, their number more than tripled, increasing from 327,000 in 1970 to 1.1 million in 1980, and their percentage share of the total number of two-person households increased from 33.0 percent to 49.2 percent. While in 1970 this phenomenon was mainly the province of older households, the critical mass, in terms of absolute numbers, has shifted to the younger-age cohorts. But this is not merely a minor fashion for America's young adults. The 25-to-44-years-of-age category accounts for 47.2 percent (537,000) of the households of this genre, the largest single concentration.

While the rate of increase has been remarkable for the latter living arrangement, it should be emphasized that they account for only 5.5 percent of all nonfamily households (1.1 million out of 20.7 million), and are outnumbered by single-person households by almost sixteen to one (17.8 million to 1.1 million).

EXHIBIT 14

Two-Person Primary Individual Households by Age: 1970 to 1980
(Numbers in Thousands)

Age (in years) of Householder (Primary Individual)	1970* Households of Two Unrelated Adults	1970* Childless Unmarried Couples Number	1970* Childless Unmarried Couples Percent	1980** Households of Two Unrelated Adults	1980** Childless Unmarried Couples Number	1980** Childless Unmarried Couples Percent
Total	991	327	33.0	2,308	1,136	49.2
Under 25	270	29	10.7	804	305	37.9
25 to 44	257	60	23.3	1,021	537	52.6
45 to 64	231	123	53.2	292	178	61.0
65 and over	234	115	49.1	192	116	60.4

Notes: *As of April.
**As of March.
[1]Non-institutional population excluding Armed Forces in barracks.
[2]Numbers may not add due to rounding.

Sources: U.S. Bureau of the Census, 1970 Census of Population, Vol. II, 4P, *Persons by Family Characteristics;* and U.S. Bureau of the Census, Current Population Reports, series P-20, No. 365, *Marital Status and Living Arrangements: March 1980,* U.S. Government Printing Office, Washington, D.C., 1981.

FEMALE FAMILY HEADS

Exhibit 15 presents the marital status of female family heads for 1960, 1970 and 1980. While the group as a whole (excluding "husband present") increased 33.0 percent in the initial decade of this period, the increase was even larger, 53.0 percent, in the subsequent decade. Divorce on a proportionate base has played a major role with an increment of 79.2 percent in

EXHIBIT 15

Marital Status of Female Family Heads: 1960 to 1980

(Numbers in Thousands)

	1960	1970	1980	Percent Change 1960-1970	Percent Change 1970-1980
All Female Family Heads	4,196	5,580	10,171	33.0	NA
Single	487	610	1,328	25.3	117.7
Married, Husband Present*	—	—	1,631	—	—
Married, Husband Absent	914	1,324	1,734	44.9	31.0
Widowed	2,093	2,389	2,518	14.1	5.4
Divorced	702	1,258	2,961	79.2	135.4
Female Family Heads, excluding Married, Husband Present*	4,196	5,580	8,540	33.0	53.0
White Female Family Heads	3,306	4,185	7,340	26.6	NA
White Female Family Heads excluding Married, Husband Present*	3,306	4,185	5,963	26.6	42.5
Black Female Family Heads	890	1,349	2,649	51.6	NA
Black Female Family Heads excluding Married, Husband Present*	890	1,349	2,429	51.6	80.1

Notes: *,NA: Prior to 1980, the husband in a married-couple household was always considered to be the "householder" or "head of household." Beginning in 1980, either the husband or the wife was listed as householder.
[1]Non-institutional population, excluding Armed Forces in barracks.
[2]Numbers may not add due to rounding.

Sources: U.S. Bureau of the Census, Current Population Reports, Series P-20, No. 307, *Population Profile of the United States: 1976,* U.S. Government Printing Office, Washington, D.C., 1977; and U.S. Bureau of the Census, Current Population Reports, Series P-20, No. 365, *Marital Status and Living Arrangements: March 1980,* U.S. Government Printing Office, Washington, D.C., 1981.

the 1960s and 135.4 percent in the subsequent decade. The second most striking gain was in the group of single women who, between 1970 and 1980, increased in number by 117.7 percent.

Some of these shifts may well be more in the nature of step functions than dynamic in nature, as, for example, the rise in divorce occasioned by the rise of simplified no-fault approaches within local law. And similarly new opportunities for women may make single status as head of household more economically feasible.

Regardless of the forces at work, however, they are unequally shared when they are analyzed by racial characteristics as shown at the bottom of Exhibit 15. The 1970 to 1980 growth rate of white female family heads (excluding "husband present") was 42.5 percent — the equivalent for black female family heads, 80.1 percent. While the two diverse proportions show some signs of narrowing, to the degree that female-headed households tend to have relatively low incomes — if not to be in poverty status — their increase in numbers is most ominous for social planners. Much of the absolute growth is the residual of broken families; some of it, however, represents the increased proportion of women who have never been married.

SINGLE (NEVER MARRIED) WOMEN

Irrespective of their household and family-membership status, the proportion of women remaining single is experiencing a substantial upswing. As shown in Exhibit 16 this is particularly characteristic of the more youthful women of our society. In 1980, the proportion of women 20 to 24 years of age who had never married (50.2 percent) was almost twice the equivalent for 1960 (28.4 percent), with a similar evolution over time in the 25-to-29-years-of-age category. It should be pointed out that the increase in the 20-to-24-year-old sector is particularly significant since this is the age when most women have traditionally married. Moreover, in conjunction with the increased prevalence of non-marriage in the subsequent age group (25 to 29 years), it may suggest the general acceptance by young women for either postponing marriage or remaining single throughout their lives.

It is interesting to note the reverse pattern as we focus on the older age groups. In 1960 there was a far higher proportion of women, particularly in those age categories above 45 years, who had never married then holds true currently (1980). Is this the residual of trends earlier in this century in Suffragettism? Is it related in part, particularly among the middle-aged members of this group, to the depression years? Or does it perhaps indicate that in the future we will see a shift toward later marriage? And if it is the last, what impact will that have on population growth? Some light may be focused on this possibility by examining the birth expectations of wives.

EXHIBIT 16
Percent Single (Never Married) Women by Age
1960 to 1980

Age	1960	1970	1975	1980
Total, 15 years and over*	19.0	22.1	22.8	22.4
Under 40 years	NA	38.5	39.5	38.7
Over 40 years	NA	6.2	5.1	5.1
20 to 24	28.4	35.8	40.3	50.2
25 to 29	10.5	10.5	13.8	20.8
30 to 34	6.9	6.2	7.5	9.5
35 to 39	6.1	5.4	5.0	6.2
40 to 44	6.1	4.9	4.8	4.8
45 to 54	7.0	4.9	4.6	4.7
55 to 64	8.0	6.8	5.1	4.6
65 years and over	8.5	7.7	5.8	5.9

Notes: *Figures for 1960, 1970, and 1975 include persons 14 years of age.
[1]Non-institutional population excluding Armed Forces in barracks.

Source: U.S. Bureau of the Census, Current Population Reports, Series P-20, No. 365, *Marital Status and Living Arrangements: March 1980,* U.S. Government Printing Office, Washington, D.C., 1981.

BIRTH EXPECTATIONS OF WIVES

Exhibit 17 presents the birth expectations of wives according to age and race from 1967 to 1980. The data are based upon survey questions regarding how many births women of various age categories anticipate. In general, in every period it is the more youthful wives who have the lowest birth expectations. The shrinkage is substantial; in 1967 while wives aged between 18 and 24 years anticipated 2.85 births, their peers in the 30-to-34-year range were expecting approximately 3.29 births. Moreover, the decline over time for equivalent age groups is pervasive. Again the most youthful category (those 18 to 24 years of age) in 1980 anticipated a rate of only 2.13, a close approximation of zero population growth; their older peers in the 30-to-34-years-of-age sector were at the 2.25 level.

The basic patterns continue when the data are partitioned by race. While birth expectations of blacks are somewhat higher, particularly for the older age groups, they are strikingly comparable in the 18-to-24-years-of-age category (2.16 versus 2.13 in 1980). To the degree that these expectations are appropriate forecasts for the future, then, even if marriage (for the moment assumed as a preliminary to births) takes place at a later life stage, the resulting number of children will be relatively modest. And certainly this data is enhanced if we view responses of all women including those who are not

EXHIBIT 17
Birth Expectations of Currently Married Women
By Age* and Race: 1967 to 1980
(Births expected Per 1,000 Wives)

	Births expected by wives aged			
	18 to 24 years	**25 to 29 years**	**30 to 34 years**	**35 to 39 years**
Total				
1967	2,852	3,037	3,288	3,300
1975	2,173	2,260	2,610	3.058
1980	2,134	2,166	2,248	NA
White				
1967	2,859	3,001	3,200	3,215
1975	2,147	2,233	2,564	2,989
1980	2,130	2,146	2,223	NA
Black				
1967	2,787	3,407	4,257	4,226
1975	2,489	2,587	3,212	3,962
1980	2,155	2,426	2,522	NA

Note: *Age of women at survey date. Data limited to reporting women.

Source: U.S. Bureau of the Census, Current Population Reports, Series P-20, *Fertility of American Women: June 1980,* U.S. Government Printing Office, Washington, D.C., 1981.

currently married, as shown in Exhibit 18. The "all women" category by age group in general has lower expected lifetime births than holds true for the currently married. The widowed, divorced, and separated are also lower than the currently married. Certainly, then, there is no indication in the response of the singles group to indicate that there is a potential reservoir of birth augmentation to be anticipated from their ranks.

ARE TRENDS DESTINY?

One of the few definitive propositions that have emerged from social-science research would deny any all-inclusive affirmative response to the rhetorical question posed in this subtitle. It is equally evident, however, that long-term phenomena of substantial sweep must be given considerable weight as we attempt to view the future. In this context, the secular birth-rate evolution (the number of live births per 1,000 total population) from 1820 to

EXHIBIT 18

Births to Date and Lifetime Births Expected Per 1,000 Women by Martial Status: 1980

	All Women		Currently Married (Except Separated)		Widowed, Divorced and Separated		Single	
Age	Births to Date	Lifetime Births Expected	Births to Date	Lifetime Births Expected	Births to Date	Lifetime Births Expected	Births to Date	Lifetime Births Expected
18 to 24	479	1,117	846	2,134	1,183	1,952	165	343
25 to 29	1,237	2,022	1,402	2,166	1,440	1,898	422	1,529
30 to 34	1,905	2,149	2,017	2,248	2,015	2,196	670	1,161

Notes: Data limited to reporting women.

Source: U.S. Bureau of the Census, Current Population Reports, Series P-20, *Fertility of American Women: June 1980,* U.S. Government Printing Office, Washington, D.C., 1981.

1980 deserves careful study (Exhibit 19). The first 100 years of the period saw a steady decline, from the 55.2 level of 1820 to half of that (27.7) in 1920. The 1940 rate of 19.4 represents a downward acceleration compared to the gradual lessening of the earlier periods, a measure of the extraordinary circumstances of the Depression. What is more significant, however, is the explosion of the birth rate in 1947 (to the 26.6 level) and the subsequent resumption of the long-term pattern of decline after that date. It is indeed possible to view the immediate post-World War II baby boom as a short-term aberrant compensating for depression-era deficits without necesarily invalidating the century-long secular trend.

In the mixed context of the recent (1960 through 1976) acceleration of decline (38 percent in 16 years), i.e., the long-term dynamic, and the slight upward shift post-1976, what should we expect in the future? Certainly the sharp downturn of the decade of the 1930s, and the compensating upsurge in 1947, could provide the logic for predicting an analogous self-corrective to occur in the short-term future. What such a scenario could imply would be a temporary upswing to the long-term trend and then the subsequent resumption of slow but continuously declining birth rates.

What may disrupt this scenario, however, is an equivalent to the severe economic and social dislocations of the depression and World War II —

EXHIBIT 19

The Secular Trendline

Total Birth Rate[1]: 1820-1980

Year	Rate
1820	55.2
1840	51.8
1860	44.3
1880	39.8
1900	32.3
1920	27.7
1940	19.4
1947	26.6
1960	23.7
1970	18.4
1975	14.8
1976	14.8
1977	15.4
1978	15.3
1979	15.9
1980	16.2

Note: [1]Number of live births per 1,000 total population.

Source: U.S National Center for Health Statistics, *Vital Statistics of the United States,* annual.

which underlay the distorted birth rates of 1940 and 1947. While our own era has its share of trauma (the recessions of 1975 and 1982, for example), we may hope that they will not match the disruptive magnitude of the early events. And even the latter, despite their severity, were only temporary in terms of the long sweep of history.

We would hazard the assertion that there are no equivalent traumas underlying recent events, and that any *sharp* deviation in the long trend of modest levels of fertility is unlikely in their absence. To cause a significant shift in the social and cultural forces that affect the birth rate will probably require threshold changes on the order of those prevalent from 1930 to 1945. The forces presently in motion — the maturation of the women's movement, contraception, and abortion, for example — also appear not to be temporary, but on the verge of permanent institutionalization. The labor and work force parameters of the following section also provide backing for this assumption.

Consequently the extrapolation of a long-term secular trend — of gradual and perhaps decreasing declines — stands as our expectation for the short-term future. However, slight but temporary upward fluctuations remain a distinct possibility. Because of the large number of women of child-bearing age, this could cause the resulting output to be considerable in magnitude.

There is perhaps one certainty in our hesitant prognostications — their validity can be evaluated very quickly. The initial and oldest products of the baby boom are now over 30 years of age. Since it is desirable for women to have children before the age of 35, the birth rate of the over-30 group in the next several years will be a key lead indicator of the future. If there is no significant increase through the early 1980s, the probability of the continuation of the present trendline will be very high.[12]

FUTURE HOUSEHOLD PATTERNS

In this context, Census Bureau projections of households to 1990 reflect in general a demographic extension of the preceding decade (1970 to 1980) in terms of overall magnitude and broad contours. However, as a function of the aging of the baby-boom and baby-bust generations, married-couple families will bulk larger in the 1980-to-1990 growth increment, and nonfamily household somewhat smaller, as compared to the 1970s — with the latter a function of the decline in the number of individuals (baby bust) entering into the age span of initial household formation.

Facilitating this demographic evolution are the labor-force patterns described in the following two chapters. However, the economic parameters of the 1980s may well serve to retard the relative ease of household formation that was so characteristic of the 1970s, rendering the expectations encompassed by Exhibit 20 somewhat optimistic. Potential economic, income, consumption, and housing strictures in this regard are reviewed in chapters 6 through 9.

EXHIBIT 20
Household Projections: 1990
(Numbers in Thousands)

	1970	1980	Change: 1970-1980 Number	Change: 1970-1980 Percent	1990	Change: 1980-1990 Number	Change: 1980-1990 Percent
Total	63,401	79,108	15,707	24.8%	96,653	17,545	22.2%
Family Households	51,456	58,426	6,970	13.5	68,488	10,062	17.2
Married Couple Family	44,728	48,180	3,452	7.7	54,731	6,551	13.6
Male Householder[2]	1,228	1,706	478	38.9	2,185	479	28.1
Female Householder[2]	5,500	8,540	3,040	55.3	11,572	3,032	35.5
Non-family Households	11,945	20,682	8,737	73.1	28,166	7,484	36.2

Notes: [1]Series B Projection; numbers may not add due to rounding.
[2]No spouse present.

Source: U.S. Department of Commerce, Bureau of the Census, Current Population Reports, Series P-25, No. 805, *Projections of the Number of Households and Families: 1979 to 1995,* U.S. Government Printing Office, Washington, D.C., 1979.

SUMMARY

The American household has undergone a basic transformation as the currents of social change assumed new directions. The following is a summary of the more pertinent parameters attendant on these phenomena.

1. The most visible manifestation of the evolving household of America is its reduction in scale. Between 1950 and 1980, it declined slowly but consistently from an average size of 3.37 persons to 2.75 persons.
   a. A key input into this contraction is the declining fertility rate specified earlier, and the increasing rate of childlessness among young married women.
   b. Another major factor comprises fundamental changes in the marriage relationship. The divorce rate has more than doubled over the past 15 years, while the age at marriage has increased. There is some indication that a general pattern of postponing marriage is an increasingly prevalent norm for young women.
2. Subsumed under the cloak of the household-size transformation are the changing formats of the nation's households. The traditional husband and wife (married couple) module by itself is no longer a sufficient descriptor. A new typology has to be formulated.
   a. Married couple families accounted for three-quarters of America's households in 1960; by 1980, their share declined to below three-fifths. In the 1970 to 1980 period, they were the slowest-growing household type (7.7 percent).
   b. In contrast, female family heads (female householder, other family) increased 55.3 percent since 1970. Families headed by women (no spouse present), then, represent a growing proportion of America's households. For the most part, this change has largely resulted from the increasing divorce rate.
   c. Nonfamily households have experienced a remarkable growth surge over the past 20 years, accounting for 26.1 percent of all households in 1980 (compared to 15.0 percent in 1960). In 1980, 86 percent of nonfamily households comprised a single person.
   d. The other nonfamily category, comprising two or more nonrelatives, was the fastest-growing household type, increasing by 16.2 percent between 1970 and 1980.
   e. Although their absolute number is small (1.1 million in 1980), childless unmarried couples represent the fastest expanding living arrangement in the nation with their ranks more than tripling in the past ten years.
3. These new conventions are reflected by declining birth expectations, particularly among the younger age cohorts, not only of married wives, but of single, widowed, divorced, and separated women.
4. In an era of decreasing shelter-buying power, do the new formats of the

American household (particularly as they imply a diminished importance for child-oriented families) portend the emergence of a new base upon which to hinge the revitalization of America's troubled central cities? Can the first generation spawned and reared in the nation's suburbs be lured back to remnants of a previous age? Will the cities be able to marshall their resources to meet the challenge of the ostensible opportunities?

5. Despite the heroic efforts of the past, it is difficult to refute the paucity of success in deflecting the downward trends of the urban centers of America. Yet the age structure shifts of the 35 years following World War II virtually dictated the emergence of mass suburbia, overwhelming most central-city initiatives. With the new age structure and household patterns at least part of the rationale for suburbia is removed. Is the time at hand when efforts at revitalizing central cities will be congruent with the social trends? It will indeed be paradoxical if a resurgence of urban living occurs just as the national commitment to cities has virtually disintegrated.
6. This leads to the question of broad housing demand. While age-structure shifts imply a single-family boom, the household transformation may dampen this possibility, at least if the soaring housing-cost variable is entered into the equation. One important factor in this context has been the desire for single-family units by smaller households, even if they lack children. There are indications that this may well be the rule rather than the exception.
7. Despite, or perhaps as a consequence of, soaring housing costs, the single-family unit has been the major inflationary proof vehicle available to most Americans. If housing is viewed not strictly in terms of shelter functions but in reference to investment and capital accumulation criteria, then the rationale for single-family units remains, whatever contractions occur in child-rearing pressures. Yet before definitive conclusions can be risked, labor-force and employment variables must be reviewed.

Chapter Four

POPULATION AND LABOR FORCE GROWTH PATTERNS

Changes in fertility rates, their reflection in diminished population growth and shifting age structures, and their interrelationship with evolving household configurations do not occur without corresponding changes in the patterns of labor-force participation. Yet it is probably impossible to suggest which variable is causal. Do lower fertility rates enable more women to enter the labor force, thereby attaining the means to establish separate households? Or do increased consumption requirements necessitate women entering the labor force, thereby causing reduced fertility rates? To view the problem in terms of discrete linear causal relationships is futile. America's changing population landscape is the product of a number of factors interacting with and reinforcing one another, eventually coalescing into a dynamic whose surface at best is described by the data available.

Certainly, however, a corollary of the changes already described is the emerging labor-force and employment patterns of individuals and households. The former will be the focus of the immediate discussion, while the latter will be reserved for the following section.

Changes in the Gross National Product (chapter 6), of unemployment, and of many aspects of social-service delivery requirements are strongly influenced by changes in the scale and composition of the labor force itself. As we shall note later, alterations in the labor force, though linked to variations in the size of the population of working age, are far from directly determined by it. The shifts in participation rates of people of both sexes in specific age groups have been more consequential than the absolute growth of the particular age cohorts.[13]

POPULATION AND LABOR FORCE

Exhibit 21 presents the growth of the noninstitutional working-age population (16 years of age and over) and the civilian labor force from 1950 to 1980.

EXHIBIT 21
Population and Labor Force: 1950 to 1980
(Numbers in Thousands)

	Total Noninstitutional Population[1]	Civilian Labor Force		
		Total	Male	Female
1950	106,645	62,208	43,819	18,389
1955	112,732	65,023	44,475	20,548
1960	119,759	69,628	46,388	23,240
1965	129,236	74,455	48,255	26,200
1970	140,182	82,715	51,195	31,520
1975	153,448	92,613	55,615	36,998
1980	166,246	104,719	60,145	44,574
Percent Increase				
1950-1980	55.9	68.3	37.3	142.4

Note: [1] 16 years of age and over.

Source: U.S. Department of Labor, Bureau of Labor Statistics, *Employment and Earnings,* Monthly.

Over the long term (1950 to 1980), while the noninstitutional population increased by 55.9 percent, the labor force increased by 68.3 percent. Indeed, if the labor-force participation rate was the same in 1980 as in 1950 (58.3 percent), there would be 95.7 million people in the labor force instead of the actual total of 104.7 million — and hypothetically — negative unemployment.

As is evident, the key differential is the product of the increased participation in the labor force of American women (Exhibit 22). Their ranks swelled by 142.4 percent over the 30-year period, over twice as fast as the population increase and almost four times as fast as the growth rate of males (37.3 percent) in the labor force.

The impetus for this phenomenon takes many forms — the women's movement, the changing pattern of occupations in a post-industrial society (whereby many of today's jobs can be handled by either sex), the introduction of labor saving devices and conveniences in the home (providing emancipation from historical housewife functions), and changing cost of living parameters (or consumption requirements and desires). While these latter elements are the focus of chapters 6 through 10, whatever interacting causal forces are operative, it is clear that the phenomenon represents not a temporary surge, but a long term reality.

EXHIBIT 22
Women in the Labor Force[1]
(Numbers in Thousands)

	Female Population[1] 16 Years and Over	Those in Civilian Labor Force	Percent in Labor Force
1950	54,293	18,389	33.9
1955	57,610	20,548	35.7
1960	61,615	23,240	37.7
1965	66,763	26,200	39.2
1970	72,774	31,520	43.3
1975	79,954	36,998	46.3
1980	86,604	44,574	51.5
		Percent Increase	
1950-1980	59.5	142.4	—
1970-1980	19.0	41.4	—

Note: [1]Non-institutional population.
Source: U.S. Department of Labor, Bureau of Labor Statistics, *Employment and Earnings,* Monthly.

WOMEN IN THE LABOR FORCE

The vigorous advance of female participation in the labor force is detailed in Exhibit 22. In 1950, approximately one-third (33.9 percent) of the female population 16-years-of-age and over were in the civilian labor force. By 1980, it was more than one out of two (51.5 percent), and this despite the diversion of the female population increasingly into forms of higher education, and the comparatively small number of working women 65-years-of-age and over.

The profile of growth is not limited to younger women — it is pervasive across all age categories. Exhibit 23 details the transformation between 1947 and 1980. In the former year, the pattern is one of heavy participation in the 20 to 24 year old category (45 percent), a diminishment in the earlier years of child-bearing (25 to 34 years) to the 32 percent level, a slight increase for the 35 to 44 years of age category (36 percent), with declines evident for subsequent cohorts. The 1980 profile indicates a substantial growth enhancement for

EXHIBIT 23
Select Age Group Characteristics—Labor Force Participation Rates: 1947 to 1980

	Women in Labor Force (Rate)	
Age Group	**1947**	**1980**
20 to 24 Years	44.9%	69.0%
25 to 34 Years	32.0	65.4
35 to 44 Years	36.3	65.5
45 to 54 Years	32.7	59.9
55 to 64 Years	24.3	41.5
65 Years and Over	8.1	8.1
	Males in Labor Force (Rate)	
	1947	**1980**
45 to 54 Years	95.5%	91.2%
55 to 64 Years	89.6	72.3
65 Years and Over	47.8	19.1

Source: U.S. Department of Labor, Bureau of Labor Statistics, *Employment and Earnings,* Monthly.

every age classification. Indeed, at the 20-to-24-years-of age-level, more than two out of three women (69 percent) are in the labor force. Moreover, the prevalence of higher education opportunities have probably acted as a retardant to even more dramatic growth. Consequently, the largest changes over time are among older women.

To the degree that these changes are a function of shifts in occupation to those which are performed equally well among the sexes (with paper work, for example, replacing physical labor), male workers face increasing competition. Perhaps one of its manifestations is symbolized by the many men who are dropping out of the labor force into early retirement. As shown at the bottom of Exhibit 23, the labor-force participation rate of older males has declined sharply over the past 33 years. In 1947, almost half (47.8 percent) of the nation's males 65 years of age and over were still in the labor force. Presently (1980), only one-fifth (19.1 percent) of the equivalent group are still active participants. Equally significant, although smaller in magnitude, is the decline for men 55 to 64 years of age. To what extent, then, are the female inroads linked to the male demise? While we are unable to answer this question, the fact that almost half (48.4 percent) of the females of working age are not in the labor force (perhaps representing potential for future increase) makes its answer a vital concern for future public policy, particularly since the nation is now experiencing rapid growth in the 25-to-44-years-of-age population, detailed earlier in the age structure discussion (chapter 2).

AN INTERNATIONAL COMPARISON

The ultimate effect of ebullient female-labor-force participation in the United States was detailed in Exhibit 21: a massive growth surge in this nation's labor force. This phenomenon, along with rapid growth in the working age population, is relatively unique in a broader context. As shown in Exhibit 24, the growth of the United States' labor force between 1969 and 1979 was three times as fast as Japan's (27.5 percent versus 9.8 percent) and four and one half times in absolute increment. What is equally striking is the stagnation and actual decline in size of West Germany's labor force.

An added perspective on the American situation can be secured by comparing Exhibit 24 to the comparative working age (15 to 64 years) population statistics of Exhibit 9 (chapter 2). In Japan and West Germany, the absolute growth in the labor force was considerably smaller than the gains in working-age population. In the United States, however, the labor-force expansion exceeded the growth in working age population. While the directions of causality are complex, the American phenomenon occurred at a time of less than stellar economic performance — as compared to Japan and West Germany, and indeed may be linked to it (see chapter 6). The stresses emanating from job demand, labor-force growth, and stagflation as we move deeper into the 1980s are far from a clear-cut resolution.

THE FUTURE

The continued expansion of the female labor force is the basic scenario drawn by the U.S. Department of Labor through 1990. As detailed in Exhibit

EXHIBIT 24

1969 to 1979 Comparative Labor Force Growth: United States, West Germany and Japan
(Numbers in Thousands)

	Labor Force (Civilian)			Change: 1969-1979	
	1969	1974	1979	Number	Percent
United States	80,733	91,011	102,908	22,175	27.5%
West Germany	26,050	26,270	25,917	-133	-0.5
Japan[1]	50,980	53,100	55,960	4,980	9.8

Note: [1]Total labor force.
Source: OECD (Organization for Economic Cooperation and Development), Labor Force Statistics: 1968-1979, Paris, 1981.

25, female labor force participation rates in the 1980s are predicted to continue the pace of increase demonstrated over the past generation. In conjunction with working age population growth (chapter 2), this will assure substantial and sustained labor-force growth through the 1980s (Exhibit 26). Although a somewhat diminished rate of expansion will be extant — a result of the baby bust supplanting the baby boom — the absolute growth in the 1980s (18 million new labor-force participants as compared to the 1970s' 22 million) will scarcely diminish the pressures of sustaining a high level of job creation.

SUMMARY

The evolution of the United States into a post-industrial economy in the past quarter century has been accompanied by dramatic increases in the size of the labor force. The mythology of a leisure society is giving way to the reality of an adult work society.

1. While the working-age population of America increased by 55.9 percent from 1950 to 1980, the labor force increased by 68.3 percent.
2. With early retirement increasingly common, this differential emerged despite the fact of sharp declines in the labor-force-participation rates of

EXHIBIT 25

Select Age Group Characteristics:
Projections of Labor Force Participation Rates — 1990[1]

	Women in Labor Force (Rate)	
Age Group	**1980**	**1990**
20 to 24 Years	69.0%	81.4%
25 to 34 Years	65.4	80.7
35 to 44 Years	65.5	78.6
45 to 54 Years	59.9	64.3
55 to 64 Years	41.5	41.7
65 Years and Over	8.1	7.3
	Males in Labor Force (Rate)	
	1980	**1990**
45 to 54 Years	91.2%	90.8%
55 to 64 Years	72.3	67.5
65 Years and Over	19.1	15.8

Note: [1]Middle-growth projection.

Source: Howard N. Fullerton, Jr., "The 1995 Labor Force: A First Look," *Monthly Labor Review*, December, 1980.

EXHIBIT 26
Population and Labor Force Projections[1]
1980 to 1995
(Numbers in Thousands)

Year	Total Noninstitutional Population[2]	Civilian Labor Force Total	Male	Female
1980	164,144	104,719	60,145	44,574
1985	172,850	114,985	63,600	51,385
1990	180,129	122,375	65,880	56,495
Percent Increase				
1970-1980[3]	17.1%	26.6	17.5	41.4
1980-1990	9.7	16.9	9.5	26.7

Notes: [1]Middle-growth projection.
[2]16 years of age and over.
[3]Calculated from Exhibit 21.

Source: Howard N. Fullerton, Jr., "The 1995 Labor Force: A First Look," *Monthly Labor Review*, December, 1980.

men over the age of 55. Indeed, the male component of the labor force actually did not keep pace with population growth, increasing by only 37.3 percent from 1950 to 1980.

3. In contrast, the rapid expansion of the female labor force (142.4 percent over the past 30 years) appears as one of the more striking events of recent history. The labor-force-participation rate of women increased from 33.9 percent in 1950 to 51.6 percent in 1980.

The implications of this phenomenon by itself are myriad, not the least of them is reflected in the substantial increase in unemployment throughout the late 1970s and early 1980s. Moreover, given the changing age structure of America and the rapid accession of the baby-boom residuals into the labor force — as well as the unknown dimension of illegal immigration — the American economy is severely strained to provide full employment. In addition, the competition presently facing our minority-group citizenry in this context cannot be minimized. But other repercussions are amplified as they manifest themselves within the family unit.

Chapter Five

FAMILY AND EMPLOYMENT CHARACTERISTICS

The mutually reinforcing character of social events, the push versus the pull factors and their coalescence defy casual analysis. When we turn to the tremendous changes that have taken place in the employment characteristics of husband-and-wife households, certainly this dilemma becomes evident. How do we quantify the role of inflation in making the burden of maintaining a standard of living so onerous as to require multiple wage earners? Of the current escalation in housing costs in encouraging both husband and wife to participate in the labor force? Of the role of feminine awareness? Of a new consciousness of the necessity to have independent economic incomes as marriage becomes more transient? These and a host of other factors obviously play a role in the dynamics underlying the data presented in this chapter. Regardless of the causal elements, the results are at hand — their influence of enormous import in the present and future patterns of development within the United States.

SPOUSES WORKING AND IN THE LABOR FORCE

The events documented in the previous section cannot be attributed to the soaring divorce rates and the demise of marriage rates detailed earlier. The pattern of working women is even more pronounced as husband-wife families are examined. Exhibit 27 indicates that the number of employed husbands in husband-wife families increased by 32.2 percent for the 33 years from April 1947 to March 1980. In the equivalent period, the number of employed wives grew by 276.1 percent, nearly ten times as fast. Despite the relatively low base level for the latter group, the absolute increment in the number of employed wives (18 million) was nearly double the gain in number of employed husbands.

EXHIBIT 27

Working Spouses: 1947 to 1980[1]

(Numbers in Thousands)

Date	Employed Husbands	Employed Wives
April 1947	29,865	6,502
March 1980	39,473	24,456
1947 to 1980 Percent Change	32.2%	276.1%

Note: [1]Husband or Wife employed, spouse present; 16 years of age and over beginning 1967; 14 years of age and over until 1967.

Source: U.S. Department of Labor and U.S. Department of Health, Education, and Welfare, *Employment and Training Report of the President,* U.S. Government Printing Office, Washington, D.C., 1977; U.S. Department of Commerce, Bureau of the Census, Current Population Reports, Series P-20, No. 363, *Population Profile of the United States: 1980,* U.S. Government Printing Office, Washington, D.C., 1981.

There were two factors at hand that account for the arithmetic — if not the phenomena: the first of these was a decline in labor force participation rates for husbands. As shown in Exhibit 28, they declined from 91.6 percent in 1950 to 81 percent in 1980. At the same time, however, the labor-force-participation rate of wives more than doubled, from the 23.8 percent level in the base year to 50.2 percent in 1980. Given the typical American pattern of husbands being older than wives, this may in part reflect the pattern of earlier retirement for the men. But nevertheless, the reality of a basic transformation is certainly obvious.

MULTIPLE-WORKER FAMILIES

It should be noted in this context that the proportion of families with two workers or more does not necessarily mean that one of those workers will be a wife. As shown in Exhibit 29, 36.1 percent of husband-wife families had two workers or more in 1950, with the labor-force-participation rate of wives only 23.8 percent. By 1980, the equivalent proportions were 53.7 and 50.1 percent respectively. While this does not necessarily imply a labor-force-participation rate reduction for non-husbands or non-wives within the household, there are indications from the previous exhibits that such individuals are decreasingly present. The formation of separate households at an earlier age by the younger generation has been influential. Again the causal linkage is obscure. As the younger generation exits, does the wife have to work so as to maintain the rent-paying capacity of the family? Or has the shift out of the household by the younger generation been made feasible by the wife/mother working? Inter-

EXHIBIT 28

Spouse in Labor Force: 1950-1980[1] (Labor Force Participation Rates)[2]

Year	Husband	Wives
1950	91.6	23.8
1955	90.7	27.7
1960	88.9	30.5
1965	87.7	34.7
1970	86.9	40.8
1975	82.8	44.4
1980	81.0	50.2

Notes: [1]Husband or wife in labor force, spouse present.
[2]Rates are for March of each year, except for 1955, which is for April.

Source: U.S. Department of Labor and U.S. Department of Health, Education, and Welfare, *Employment and Training Report of the President,* U.S. Government Printing Office, Washington, D.C., 1977; U.S. Department of Commerce, Bureau of the Census, Current Population Reports, Series P-20, No. 363, *Population Profile of the United States: 1980,* U.S. Government Printing Office, Washington, D.C., 1981.

penetrating these questions are the inclusion of elderly workers, perhaps of an older generation, within the family unit. This may have been much more common in 1950 than today, when the elderly maintain separate households of their own frequently in retirement enclaves.

Again the push-pull inputs are all too complex. Does the financial capacity

EXHIBIT 29

Trends in the Proportion of Husband-Wife Families With 2 Workers or More and the Labor Force Participation Rates of Wives: March 1950 to March 1980

Year	Proportion of Families With 2 Workers or More	Labor Force Participation Rate of Wives
1950	36.1	23.8
1955	36.2	27.7
1960	38.3	30.5
1965	41.6	34.7
1970	46.2	40.8
1975	48.7	44.4
1980	53.7	50.1

Note: March to March except for 1965, which is April.

Source: U.S. Bureau of the Census, Current Population Survey, unpublished data.

achieved by virtue of the wife working lead to the dissolution of the extended family unit, or are the dynamics behind the latter even broader — and bringing in their wake both the necessity as well as the relative freedom of the wife participating in the labor force? Obviously neither of these precludes the other —the respective shares, however, remain obscure.

Regardless of the elements at work here, the present composition (1980) from a labor-force-participation point of view of husband-wife families is shown in Exhibit 30. The single largest partition has both principals in the labor force (46 percent). Significantly, the husband is the sole participant in the labor force in less than one-third (28 percent) of America's husband-wife families. Moreover, 14 percent of the families have no one in the labor force — typically the retired though there are other phenomena subsumed in this group. The balance of the configurations are small in number.

EXHIBIT 30

Husband-Wife Families by Labor Force Status of Family Members: March, 1980

	Percent of Total
Husband and Wife in Labor Force	46
Husband Only in Labor Force	28
None in Labor Force	14
Husband and Other in Labor Force	7
Wife Only in Labor Force	3
More than One Family Member in Labor Force, Excluding Husband	1
Other Family Member Only in Labor Force	2
TOTAL	100

Source: U.S. Bureau of the Census, Current Population Survey, unpublished data.

Put at its simplest, then, more than four in ten of all "whole" families are ones in which both husband and wife are actively participating in the labor force. In only one out of three cases is the husband alone in the labor force; and in one out of seven cases, no one is in the labor force. The new family pattern of the United States, if we can reverse this data, is one in which the earlier classic module of the husband working outside of the household with the wife substantially confined within it is the minority.

This new life pattern extends even to married women with school-age children. As shown in Exhibit 31, the labor-force-participation rate of married women with such children has gone from 28.3 percent in 1950 to 61.8 percent in 1980. Indeed, it is most striking to note that this rate is substantially higher than for wives in total, reflecting the higher labor-force-participation rate of relatively youthful women—those who would have children between 6 and 17. It also indicates, however, the decline in the classic role of child-rearer

EXHIBIT 31

Married Women (Husband Present) in the Labor Force, With School Age Children[1]

Year	Labor Force Participation Rate[2]
1950	28.3
1955	34.7
1960	39.0
1965	42.7
1970	49.2
1975	52.4
1980	61.8

Notes: Children 6 to 17 years of age.
[2]As of March of the respective years.

Source: U.S Dpeartment of Labor and U.S. Department of Health, Education, and Welfare, *Employment and Training Report of the President,* U.S. Government Printing Office, Washington, D.C., 1977; U.S. Department of Commerce, Bureau of the Census, Current Population Reports, Series P-20, No. 363, *Population Profile of the United States: 1980,* U.S. Government Printing Office, Washington, D.C., 1981.

that historically devolved — though never completely — upon married women. It is relevant also that this shift has taken place without major technological or organizational adjustments (outside the home) with which to buffer the change. Indeed, the latter have tended to lag behind the basic shift. Only recently, for example, has industry begun to adapt to the potential economies of part-time labor. Within the household, however, the complement to the labor-force-participation rate is more clearly seen in the omnipresent increments in mechanized and electronic household aids.

THE INCOME DIMENSION

The results of the shifts in work and labor-force patterns within the family are mirrored by the evolving variation between the average weekly earnings for individual workers versus median family incomes (Exhibit 32). While the former grew by 343.6 percent between 1950 and 1980, the latter increased half again as much — by 533.4 percent over the same time period. And this in turn is further reflected by the growing variation in median family income as a function of the wife in the labor force. As shown in Exhibit 33, by 1980 the median family income for families with wives in the labor force was close to $27,000, while if the wife was absent from the labor force, the median income drops to the $19,000 level. Much of the new consumer affluence of the American household is a tribute to distaff monetary input.

EXHIBIT 32
Weekly Pay vs. Family Income
(In Current Dollars)

Year	Average Weekly Earnings[1]	Median Family Income
1950	$ 53	$ 3,319
1955	68	4,421
1960	81	5,620
1965	95	6,957
1970	119	9,867
1975	164	13,719
1980	235	21,023
	Percent Increase	
1950 to 1980	343.6%	533.4%

Note: [1]Gross averages, production or nonsupervisory workers on private non-agricultural payrolls.

Source: U.S. Department of Labor, Bureau of Labor Statistics, *Monthly Labor Review,* monthly; U.S. Department of Commerce, Bureau of the Census, Current Population Reports, *Money, Income and Poverty Status of Families and Persons in the U.S.,* annual.

EXHIBIT 33
Median Family Income: Presence of Wife in Labor Force: 1950 to 1980[1]
(In 1980 Dollars)

Year	Wife in Paid Labor Force	Wife Not in Paid Labor Force
1950	13,700	11,346
1960	19,197	15,358
1965	22,450	17,214
1970	26,330	19,742
1975	26,399	19,530
1980	26,879	18,972

Note: [1]Prior to 1980 data are for all primary and secondary families; for 1980, data are for all primary families only.

Source: U.S. Bureau of the Cenusus, Current Population Reports, Series P-60, *Money Income of Families and Persons in the United States,* U.S. Government Printing Office, Washington, D.C., annual.

But note that this dollar gap may be much exaggerated. It does not take into account, for example, the unpaid services typically provided by the at-home wife and which to a certain extent must now be contracted out and/or purchased. The stagnancy of the supermarket industry in the face of the burgeoning fast-food chains stands as a prototypical symptom. Furthermore, the gross data do not show the influence of federal income-tax and social-security policy — as well as the expenses which tend to parallel the work associated expenditures of wives in the labor force. Nevertheless, given this level of variation, it is difficult to see the pattern of participation being reversed. Personal expenditure patterns in the United States tend to have a one-way ratchet providing for their continual progression. The family making $26,879 (the median family income when wives are in the paid labor force in 1980), would have considerable difficulty, both psychic as well as fiscal, in moving down to the $18,972 level (that for families with wives not in the paid labor force). Assuming that job opportunities continue to expand in quality as well as in number for women, there is little reason to believe that the trends evident here will not continue in the future. And with them, certainly the number of children, desired or practicable, must of necessity be constrained, thus perpetuating the patterns of recent history.

SUMMARY

The primary married couple family of America, an institution increasingly facing challenge from alternative household configurations, is nonetheless gaining economic validity as the nation's citizenry seek to cope with the strictures and opportunities of a more challenging economic and fiscal environment.

1. The pattern of working women, documented earlier, is further accentuated in husband-wife families. Over the past 33 years, the number of working wives (whose husband is present), increased by 276.1 percent; the husband equivalent expanded by only 32.2 percent.
2. The past 30 years saw the labor-force-participation rate of wives increase from 23.8 percent to 50.2 percent. Concurrently, that of husbands contracted from 91.6 percent to 81.0 percent, the statistical complement of changing retirement patterns.
3. Multiple-worker families are becoming the norm in America; by 1980, 53.7 percent, more than half, of the nation's families had two workers or more. Surprisingly, only in a distinct minority (28 percent) was the husband alone employed.
4. This broader phenomenon is evident regardless of realities of child-rearing responsibility. The labor-force-participation rate of wives (husband present) with school-aged children has doubled in the past three decades to a definitive majority — 61.8 percent.

5. Whatever the social and cultural implications for the traditional web of family ties and interrelationships, the economic consequences are manifold. While average weekly earnings have increased by 343.6 percent in the past 30 years, median family incomes have soared by 533.4 percent over the equivalent span of time.
6. And within the family, the economic implications of multiple workers is equally significant. In 1980, the median income of families with the wife in the paid labor force was $26,879; when the wife is absent from the labor force, the median family income falls to $18,972.
7. The very strength of these economic realities generates a net additive impetus to the process of household transformation. Certainly, it is paralleled and underscored by the rapid growth of unmarried couples noted in chapter 3.
8. At the very least, "going it alone" may be economically hazardous. Are we witnessing a fundamental bifurcation in economic capacity between multiple-worker households and their single-worker counterparts, even at equivalent occupational and social status? Does the multiple-worker format insure entry into the good life? This question will be examined in more detail in chapter 7. Before that, however, the capacity of the American economic system to deliver growth and jobs must be viewed.

Chapter Six

THE ECONOMIC ENVIRONMENT

The complex flows of influence and the levels of connection between demographics and the economy are still being explicated. The state of analytical sophistication is relatively primitive. Based upon United States history of the 1930s, we know that recessions have been accompanied, with short time lags, by declines in fertility. Whether the reverse holds true, i.e., does prosperity always lead to augmented births, or even whether earlier experiences of the linkages between economic downturns and births will hold in the future, remains to be seen.

In viewing the enormous labor-force changes which have taken place over the last generation, we must take into account the matrix of the economy in which it occurred — and certainly which was altered by its dynamic. The ebullient demographics of the baby boom, inspired by the limitations of the era which proceeded them, in turn quickened the pace of business activity — and created a buoyant atmosphere which fed back on personal incomes, the very capacity to support children and for that matter, changed life-style as well.

The issues of whether the rear guard of the baby boom, as we move into a less expansive economic era, will find equivalent opportunity — or even whether there will be the capacity to advance for the great wave of that cohort as it ages — has attracted much discussion. This chapter presents some of the basic parameters which help both to define the past as well as give some boundary conditions for the future.

THE PATTERN OF GROSS NATIONAL PRODUCT

The Gross National Product (GNP) gauges the total national output of all the nation's goods and services, encompassing personal-consumption expenditures, gross private domestic investment, net exports of goods and services, and government purchases. As such, it represents the broadest indicator of the nation's economy, measuring the output attributable to the factors of production — labor and property. It may not define changes in the quality of life such as environmental conditions and certainly it has other limitations as well — but as a first departure, it still remains a critical measuring stick. The pattern which is shown in Exhibit 34, both in current and in constant 1972 dollars, is the broad skeletal structure of resource and opportunity, of resource and limitation, within which the individual segments of industry and of individuals seek their priority niches.

The average annual percent change (in constant dollars) from 1955 to 1960 was a relatively modest but positive 2.4 percent. In the following decade, the GNP advanced at a much more vigorous rate, averaging approximately 3.9 percent per year for the entire decade. This pattern of progress, however, terminated in 1973. The issues of whether the oil crunch — and the massive structural readjustments which were to ensue — merely signaled the pattern of a start/stop economy which was to follow — or was central to its creation, will

EXHIBIT 34

Gross National Product: 1960 to 1980

(Billions of Dollars)

	Current Dollars		**Constant 1972 Dollars**	
	GNP	**Average Annual Percent Change**[1]	**GNP**	**Average Annual Percent Change**[1]
1960	$ 506	4.0%	$ 737	2.4%
1965	688	6.3	926	4.7
1970	982	7.4	1,075	3.0
1971	1,063	8.2	1,107	3.0
1972	1,171	10.2	1,171	5.8
1973	1,307	11.6	1,235	5.5
1974	1,413	8.1	1,218	-1.4
1975	1,529	8.2	1,202	-1.3
1976	1,718	12.4	1,300	8.2
1977	1,918	11.6	1,372	5.5
1978	2,156	12.4	1,437	4.7
1979	2,414	12.0	1,483	3.2
1980	2,626	8.8	1,481	-0.1
1981	2,925	11.4	1,510	2.0

Notes: [1]Change from prior year; for 1960, 1965 and 1970, average annual change for preceding five years.

Source: U.S. Department of Commerce, Bureau of Economic Analysis, *The National Income and Product Accounts of the United States, 1929-74: Survey of Current Business,* July issues and March, 1981.

be debated for generations to come (see chapter 7). In any case, the years that immediately followed were ones marked by a very sharp recession, a nearly equally abrupt pinnacle of recovery (in 1976) followed by a slow but steady decline to the negative levels which dominated in 1980 and 1981.

The generation-long mood of national confidence, though periodically punctuated by mild rolling recessions, has seemingly come to a sudden halt with the erratic results of the latter 1970s. It is not much more than ten years ago when the economics profession gloried in the thought that the business cycle, long the bane of economic existence, had finally been "cured" — the sole remaining issues of the profession were to be devoted to "fine tuning." Additional experience unfortunately has left this presumption lying in the dust.

The internal vagaries of the last several years, as illustrated in Exhibit 35, are reminiscent of a car which has a problem with stalling: repeated signals seemingly of the economy moving forward — only to slip into a negative

EXHIBIT 35
Gross National Product by Quarter: 1979-1981
(Billions of 1972 Dollars)

Year and Quarter	GNP (Constant 1972 Dollars)	Percent Change From Previous Quarter
1979		
I	$1,479.9	1.0
II	1,473.4	-0.4
III	1,488.2	1.0
IV	1,490.6	0.2
1980		
I	$1,501.9	0.8
II	1,463.3	-2.6
III	1,471.9	0.6
IV	1,485.6	0.9
1981		
I	$1,516.4	2.1
II	1,510.4	-0.4
III	1,515.8	0.0
IV	1,497.6	-1.2

Source: U.S. Department of Commerce, Bureau of Economic Analysis, *Survey of Current Business,* monthly.

posture. The dilemma of relative stagnancy in the economy linked to high levels of inflation (see Exhibit 55, chapter 9), which spawned the mid-1970s' buzz-word "stagflation," is far from limited to the United States. Given our dominance, however, in a global economy, it is clear that it can only be cured on a worldwide basis if the United States becomes much more healthy economically than has been the case.

The nature of the causal mechanisms that have been at work have been reviewed intensively. The linkage between changes in the labor force, changes in productivity and changes in investment, have been the particular target of analysts. Some of these elements are illustrated in Exhibit 36. Clearly the pattern of growth in GNP has faltered while the size of the civilian labor force has continued the growth patterns of the years of prosperity. The result (discussed in more detail in terms of their market implications in chapter 8) has been a sharp decline in the rate of growth in GNP per person in the labor force. From 1965 to 1973, GNP per labor force participant increased by 12 percent; in the post-1973 years, it secured a paltry 1.6-percent gain through 1980. And preliminary data for 1981 and the first quarter of 1982 indicate that the post-oil-crunch period has actually been barely stable at best.

In essence, there are now many more workers dividing a relatively constant-sized pie. The complement of this has been the necessity for an increased number of workers per household in order to support the good life. The two-worker household increasingly has become not merely a source of luxury, but rather a necessity for sustenance at a constant, rather than augmented, level of amenity.

EXHIBIT 36

GNP Per Person in Labor Force

(Labor Force Participant)

	GNP (Billions of 1972 Dollars)	Civilian Labor Force (Millions of Persons)	GNP Per Person in Labor Force
1965	$ 926	74.5	$12,430
1970	1,075	82.7	12,998
1973	1,235	88.7	13,923
1980	1,481	104.7	14,145
		Percent Change	
1965-73	33.3%	19.1%	12.0%
1973-80	19.9	18.0	1.6

Source: U.S. Department of Commerce, Bureau of Economic Analysis, *Survey of Current Business,* monthly; U.S. Department of Labor, Bureau of Labor Statistics, *Employment and Earnings,* monthly.

GNP COMPONENTS

One of the theses that has been advanced to explain the faltering pace of the American economy has been the concept of a recent substitution of relatively inexpensive labor for relatively expensive capital investment. If this is the case, it would reverse a long pattern of enterprise in the United States, one characterized by relatively high-cost labor (certainly in terms of a world context), and relatively inexpensive investment capital and with it a capacity for continuous modernization and productivity gains.

Earlier critics frequently remarked on the failure of the United States to rehabilitate older housing, cities and neighborhoods, rather substituting new ones in their place, without comprehending the basic labor/capital cost calculus which lay behind this patterning. What are the numbers — and do they define the case?

As shown in Exhibit 37, which details the four major GNP components, certainly the years subsequent to 1973 have been marked by a sharp decline in gross private domestic investment as a percentage of GNP, while personal-consumption expenditures have absorbed an ever-increasing share of the nation's output. There are several demurrers to this generalization; the first concerns a constant dilemma in time-series analysis — the battle of the base years. For example, if one alters the benchmark year under consideration (i.e., 1973 was a peak year, 1975 a relatively deep recession) different generalizations can be made. We would suggest, however, that clearly the levels of investment have been at best on the very modest side. A second element is the increasing proportion of post-1973 investment which went into societal requirements, such as environmental protection measures and the like. A still further dilutant was, as will be noted later, an enormous increase in investment in energy production facilities which, while they have tended to stabilize America's productive capacity, have added relatively little to it. And this occurred at the same time that energy-saving adaptations absorbed substantial sums — often with limited immediate payoff. This is not to lessen the significance of these inputs but to indicate the rival demands placed upon productive investment per se.

It is intriguing to note on the far right column of Exhibit 37 the decline in government purchases of goods and services, on a relative base, which took place over the years presented. In 1965, such activity accounted for 22.7 percent of GNP. By 1980, it declined to 19.6 percent. While the vagaries of defense expenditure played a significant role, much of this is accounted for by the lessened requirements of educational infrastructure, both physical and staff, as the baby boom became absorbed.

A further thesis has been advanced that the increase in personal consumption expenditures and its partial complement, the decline in levels of personal savings, are the reflection of a disproportionate rate of household formation — spearheaded by the maturing baby boom — which has characterized

EXHIBIT 37
Gross National Product by Components: 1960 to 1980
(Billions of Dollars)

	Gross National Product	Personal Consumption Expenditure	Gross Private Domestic Investment	Net Exports of Goods and Services	Government Purchases, Goods and Services
			Current Dollars		
1965	688	430	112	8	138
1970	982	619	141	4	219
1973	1,307	810	220	7	270
1980	2,626	1,673	395	23	535
			Constant 1972 Dollars		
1965	926	558	150	8	210
1970	1,075	669	155	1	250
1973	1,235	768	207	8	253
1980	1,481	935	204	52	290
			Percent Change[1]		
1965-73	33.4	37.6	38.0	0.0	20.5
1973-80	19.9	21.7	-1.4	550.0	14.6
			Percent Distribution[1]		
1965	100.0	60.3	16.2	0.9	22.7
1973	100.0	62.1	16.7	0.6	20.4
1980	100.0	63.1	13.8	3.5	19.6

Note: [1]In constant (1972) dollars

Source: U.S. Department of Commerce, Bureau of Economic Analysis, *The National Income and Product Accounts of the United States, 1929-74; Survey of Current Business,* July issues and March, 1981.

American society. This thesis would further suggest that what we have been dealing with is a momentary surge of need reflective of a unique demographic incidence — i.e., young, newly formed households have high consumption requirements and save very little — and that this balance will right itself as the demographic profile is altered over time — as such households mature into their peak earning years, their savings rate inexorably increases.[14]

Regardless of origin, the immediacies reflect a United States whose economic proficiency is faltering — at least in large part as a function of decline in investment.

EMPLOYMENT COROLLARIES

Despite the somber elements noted above, the United States economy has performed heroically in absorbing the burgeoning baby-boom generation into the work-force. From 1969 to 1979, for example, the total U.S. population aged between 15 to 64 years increased by nearly one in four, while by way of contrast, Germany's increased at a rate of barely one-third of that. In addition, it was able to accommodate a vast change in the work-force participation rates of women. The employment tabulations documenting this phenomenon are illustrated in Exhibit 38. (Appendix B provides comparisons with Germany and Japan.) The average annual growth in nonfarm payroll employment in the United States from 1960 to 1975 was over the 1.5 million mark.[15] From 1975 to 1981, years of relative stagnation, the annual gain actually increased to close to the 2.4-million-job level. Indeed, in absolute numbers, the latter period registered a staggering employment increase approaching 15 million. There are few periods in our history which can match this increment in proportionate terms — and none in absolute number, with the possible exception of the World War II, post-depression military buildup.

Are economic problems essentially demographic? Does the vast surge of growth in the labor force "cause" a decline in relative productivity, and with it,

EXHIBIT 38

United States Total Employment Change: 1960 to 1981[1]
(Numbers in Thousands)

Total Employment

		Change: 1960-1975		Average Annual
1960	**1975**	**Number**	**Percent**	**Change**
52,073.6	75,952.8	23,879.2	46.6%	1,591.9

		Change: 1975-1981		Average Annual
1975	**1981**	**Number**	**Percent**	**Change**
75,952.8	90,209.7	14,256.2	18.8%	2,376.0

Intraperiod Growth Increments

1960-65	6,041.9
1965-70	11,911.4
1970-75	5,925.9
1975-81	14,256.2

Note: [1]Employees on non-agriculture payrolls as of March of the respective years; excludes Hawaii and Alaska.

Source: U.S. Department of Labor, Bureau of Labor Statistics, *Employment and Earnings,* monthly.

competitiveness? Are there patterns of consumption, of savings, of life-style, of household formation and work behavior which are stimulated by the demographic phenomena underlying the data presented here? And even if these changes have in turn altered American productivity, does this necessarily mean that they are commutative, i.e., that as the demographics change, the economy moves back into a more competitive mold with them? These are among the major political/economic issues of our time. Some of our own views are expressed in chapters 7 and 8.

EMPLOYMENT BY SECTORS[16]

When employment changes are viewed by sector, the crucial alteration in the shape and dimensions of the various components of the economy become evident in Exhibit 39. (See Appendix B for data on Germany and Japan). Manufacturing employment clearly is declining in relative importance, securing barely 3.4 million additional jobs between 1960 and 1981. Concurrently, private nonmanufacturing activity virtually doubled, with a growth increment in excess of 26 million jobs. The government sector advanced very rapidly from 1960 to 1975, but expansion has slowed dramatically since that time.

By 1981, only two out of nine of all nonfarm payroll jobs in the United

EXHIBIT 39

United States Employment Change
By Sector: 1960 to 1981[1]

			Change: 1960 to 1975	
	1960	1975	Number	Percent
TOTAL	52,073.6	75,952.8	23.879.2	46.6%
Manufacturing	16,725.6	18,194.9	1,469.3	8.8
Private non-manufacturing	27,058.6	42,990.6	15,932.0	58.9
Government	8,289.4	14,767.3	6,477.9	78.1
			Change: 1975 to 1980	
	1975	**1981**	**Number**	**Percent**
TOTAL	75,952.8	90,209.0	14,256.2	18.8%
Manufacturing	18,194.9	20,133.4	1,938.5	10.7
Private non-manufacturing	42,990.6	53,344.1	10,353.5	24.1
Government	14,767.3	16,731.5	1,964.2	13.3

Note: [1]Employees on non-agriculture payrolls as of March of the respective years; excludes Hawaii and Alaska.

Source: U.S. Department of Labor, Bureau of Labor Statistics, *Employment and Earnings,* monthly.

States were in manufacturing, with an even smaller proportion in government, while private nonmanufacturing accounted for nearly 60 percent of the total. It is the latter sector that encompasses the new "post-industrial" jobs which have expanded in parallel with (or facilitated) the surge of women in the labor force.

It is important in this context to view the changing composition of America's employment matrix within the parameters of a world whose dynamic in the future clearly will be ever more intimately related to levels of technology and energy. As shown in Exhibit 40, which provides an alternative, "nonconventional" partitioning of the employment base, it is these sectors which have dominated the employment growth registers from 1976 to 1981.[17] While old-line industry increased by less than 10 percent, high technology and energy achieved 32.6 percent and 43.2 percent gains, respectively; the latter two sectors also outpaced services (26.3 percent) and government (7.1 percent) on a rate basis. (For more detail on the industries subsumed under these headings as well as individual growth rates, see Appendix A.)

EXHIBIT 40

Alternative Employment Partitions: 1976 to 1981 Change

Sector	Percent Change
Old-line Industry	9.5%
High Technology	32.6
Energy	43.2
Services	26.3
Government	7.1

Note: Excludes wholesale and retail trade, includes Hawaii and Alaska.
Source: See Appendix A.

But rates of growth are not absolute levels. Over the 1976 to 1981 period, the national economy's dependence on the services sector (as defined in Appendix A) grew by nearly 7 million jobs on an absolute base.[18] But therein another dilemma arises: many of the component activities of this sector have been the least amendable to date to rationalization and productivity-increasing measures perhaps because of the large influx of inexperienced baby boomers to the service work-force. The office/marketing automation boom now underway may radically alter the relatively low productivity of this sector and thereby its labor force absorptive capacity as well.

SUMMARY

The United States economy has managed to absorb an unprecedented flow of newcomers to the labor force. Unfortunately, in recent years this has been achieved much more through a division of the productive pie., i.e., more workers for a given level of output, than by absolute growth in throughput. The first stages of the baby boom were more successfully absorbed than has held for later groups. The shifts into the growth segments of the future, the energy and high technology areas, give hope that a basis for future vigor has been established. But these segments in the absolute are still small. Bridging the uncertain future, while permitting a restructuring of America's industry to provide a more competitive base with low-cost labor sites in the less developed world, remains as the immediate challenge.

1. After an immediate recovery following the 1974-1975 recession, the annual rate of GNP growth experienced sustained deceleration. By 1980, a negative growth posture (-0.1 percent) had evolved, and an erratic stop-start patterning became a dominant characteristic of the American economy.
2. While growth in GNP faltered, the civilian labor force continued to expand at a rapid pace. From 1965 to 1973, GNP per labor-force participant grew by 12.0 percent. But from 1973 to 1980, virtual stability ensued; GNP per labor-force participant experienced a growth rate of only 1.6 percent.
3. There are now many more workers dividing a relatively constant-sized pie. The complement has been the necessity for an increased number of workers per household in order to maintain living standards.
4. When the performance of the major GNP components is examined over the 1973 to 1980 period, a sharp relative decline in gross private domestic investment is evident, while personal consumption expenditures have absorbed an increasing share of the nation's output.
5. A major thesis linking demography and the economy has revolved around the necessity to absorb large numbers of inexperienced entrants to the labor force, depressing levels of productivity. A corollary phenomenon related to declining investment — a further productivity dilutant — has been the concurrent formation of large numbers of young households with high consumption requirements and minimal proclivities to save (and hence finance investment).
6. Whether this situation will be substantially altered as the demographic profile evolves over time — as the baby-boom generation matures to its peak earning years — is a critical question facing the United States in the 1980s.
7. Despite these somber elements, the United States' economy has performed heroically in absorbing the baby-boom surge, and the vast change in the labor-force-participation rates of women, into the work force. The 1975 to 1981 period witnessed an employment increase of 15 million jobs, an increment with few parallels in the nation's history.
8. Much of this growth was accommodated by the service industry and other post-industrial economic sectors, areas which to date have been least amenable to productivity increasing measures. Again, the demographic

linkage — it is these sectors which absorbed the baby boom and the new work patterns and desires of women — remain problematical as does the future of this sector in the face of the information handling revolution.

9. But the income consequences of a faltering economy are subject to somewhat more detailed quantification. These are examined in the following chapter, and questions are raised about some prominent demographic-economic assumptions.

Chapter Seven

FAMILY INCOME: AFFLUENCE AND STAGNATION

The Toynbee paradigm of the rise and fall of civilizations requires societies to meet and surmount challenges — or face decline. Accepting that stipulation, there are elements of recent history that require reexamination. Family incomes in the United States have never recovered from the impact of the 1973 oil embargo, which initiated a sustained process of worldwide redistribution of wealth. This basic reality has been obscured by the start/stop patterning of the United States' economy, by a spurious consumer boom fueled by a housing-buying hysteria and an underlying thrust of federal deficit spending, both on and off the budget. Even if we eliminate the impact of bracket creep in draining away pretax income, the results are all too evident. While families have gloried in the increase in nominal income secured over the 1970s, the reality in terms of constant dollars has been one of stagnation. Exhibit 41 summarizes the situation.

AFFLUENCE AND STAGNATION

The years of the American Raj, of American economic dominance and post-World War II affluence are clearly evidenced by real median family-income gains of over $4,200 (in constant 1980 dollars) in the decade of the 1950s and over $5,300 in the decade of the 1960s. Thus the median family income in America increased from $11,361 in 1950 to $20,939 by 1970, a near doubling in real terms.

But the parade to affluence terminated at its peak in 1973. The median American family, which had seen its income rise to $22,346 after the first three years of the 1970s, has yet to have it quite so good again. Despite considerable fluctuations in the ensuing years, the median family income in 1980 fell to $21,023, well below the 1973 peak. The issue of whether the oil signal was

EXHIBIT 41

Median Family Income: 1950 to 1980

	Median Family Income Actual Dollars	Median Family Income Constant 1980 Dollars
1950	$ 3,319	$11,361
1960	5,620	15,637
1970	9,867	20,939
1971	10,285	20,926
1972	11,116	21,895
1973	12,051	22,346
1974	12,902	21,559
1975	13,719	21,004
1976	14,958	21,652
1977	16,009	21,769
1978	17,640	22,280
1979[1]	19,661	22,320
1980[1]	21,023	21,023
	Gains in Real Income (Constant 1980 Dollars)	
1950 to 1960	$ 4,276	37.6%
1960 to 1970	5,302	33.9
1970 to 1980	84	0.4
1970 to 1975	65	0.3
1975 to 1980	19	0.1

Notes: [1]Based on Householder Concept.

Source: U.S Bureau of the Census, Current Population Reports, Series P-60, No. 127, *Money Income and Poverty Status of Families and Persons in the U.S.: 1980* (Advance Data from the March 1981 Current Population Survey), U.S. Government Printing Office, Washington, D.C., 1981.

merely coincidental in time or rather basic to the phenomenon may be left to future generations of Ph.D. students. The reality of stagnation, however, is all too evident. The $84 real-income gain over the 1970 to 1980 period is lamentable in the context of the achievements of the previous two decades.

THE UPPER-INCOME STRATA

Much has been made of a supposed bifurcation that has taken place in American society — of the emergence of an elite immune to the travails of the average family. The relative vigor in sales of higher-priced housing in the past two years, for example, compared to the disaster that befell its more modest equivalents, may be felt to signal this event. But when data on upper-income families are reviewed in constant 1980 dollars over the past decade, the situation is far from clear cut (Exhibit 42). In 1960, for example, only 8.61 million families out of 45.5 million (18.9 percent) had incomes of $25,000 and over. By 1973 that proportion had more than doubled, reaching a peak of 41.9 percent. In that year, 23.1 million out of 55.1 million families, reached this threshold of modest affluence. In 20 years the absolute incidence of families over this threshold had tripled. But by 1980, despite a total family base that had grown to 60.3 million, the ranks of the "affluent" remained virtually stable (23.7 million), and actually declined in relative importance to 39.3 percent. Indeed, if we review the incidence of families with incomes of $50,000 and over (once again stated in constant 1980 dollars), they comprised 7.3 percent of all families in the year of the oil crisis; by 1980, their proportion had declined to 6.7 percent.

EXHIBIT 42
Upper Income Families, 1960 to 1980, Constant 1980 Dollars
(Numbers in thousands)

	1960	**1973**	**1980**
TOTAL FAMILIES	45,539	55,053	60,309
Income $25,000 and Over			
Number[1]	8,607	23,067	23,701
Percent	18.9%	41.9%	39.3%
Income $50,000 and Over			
Number[1]	N.A.	4,019	4,041
Percent	N.A.	7.3%	6.7%

Note: [1]Derived from published percent distribution.

Source: U.S. Bureau of the Census, Current Population Reports, Series P-60, No. 127, *Money Income and Poverty Status of Families and Persons in the U.S.: 1980* (Advance Data from the March 1981 Current Population Survey), U.S. Government Printing Office, Washington, D.C., 1981.

RUNNING FASTER TO STAY IN PLACE

But these data tend to cloak the dynamics of work-force expansion that was necessary in order to achieve virtual stagnation. The assertion that the good life in America increasingly requires a household economic team of two workers understates the imperatives of the situation.

Exhibit 43 provides detailing on changes both in number and in income (in

EXHIBIT 43

Families, By Type, Total and Median Family Income, 1975 and 1979

(Numbers in Thousands)

	Total Families				Median Family Income			
			Change: 1975-1979				Change: 1975-1979	
	1975[1]	1979[2]	Number	Percent	1975	1979	Number	Percent
Total	56,245	58,426	2,181	3.9%	$13,719	$19,661	$5,942	43.3%
Married Couple Families	47,318	48,180	862	1.8	14,867	21,503	6,636	44.6
Wife in Paid Labor Force	20,833	23,763	2,930	14.1	17,237	24,957	7,720	44.8
Wife Employed	19,334	22,537	3,203	16.6	17,584	25,291	7,707	43.8
Full Time	13,512	15,881	2,369	17.5	18,262	26,196	7,934	43.4
Part Time	5,821	6,657	836	14.4	16,223	23,055	6,832	42.1
Wife Unemployed	1,499	1,226	-273	-18.2	13,260	18,569	5,309	40.0
Wife Not in Paid Labor Force	26,486	24,416	-2,070	-7.8	12,752	17,750	4,998	39.2
Male Householder, No Wife Present	1,444	1,706	262	18.1	12,995	16,867	3,872	29.8
Female Householder, No Husband Present	7,482	8,540	1,058	14.1	6,844	9,927	3,083	45.0

Notes: [1]14 Years and Over.
[2]15 Years and Over.
[3]1979 Data Based on Householder Concept.

Source: U.S. Bureau of the Census, Current Population Reports, Series P-60, No. 105, *Money Income in 1975 of Families and Persons in the United States,* U.S. Government Printing Office, Washington, D.C., 1977.
1979 Data, U.S. Bureau of the Census, Advance of Publication.

current dollars) of family configurations between 1975 and 1979.* While married-couple families increased by only 862,000 (1.8 percent) over this period, this increment was the result of a 2.93 million increase (14.1 percent) in married couples with wives in the paid labor force and a 2.07 million shrinkage (-7.8 percent) in married-couple families with wives not in the labor force. And the major gains were achieved in full time employment (2.4 million or 17.5 percent) rather than part-time status (836,000 or 14.4 percent). Equally significant is the overall magnitude of the increase in married-couple families with wives employed (3.2 million) in comparison to that of single-parent families (1.3 million) — male or female householders, no wife or husband present — the configurations with lower-income potentials.

The enormous income variation as a function of family configuration and the employment status of wives is also shown in Exhibit 43. At the upper rungs of the income ladder in 1979 were married couples with wives employed full time. Their median of $26,196 contrasts sharply with the overall median family income of $19,661. The penalty of wives not in the labor force ($17,750) or of single parent status (male householder $16,867 — female householder $9,927) is all too evident.

Thus the median family's nominal dollar increase of $5,942 from 1975 to 1979 (and as we have earlier shown, this is practically all a function of inflation) was facilitated by the addition of more than 3.2 million employed wives. And it was only this structural readjustment which permitted American families in the aggregate from experiencing substantial real income declines.

THE NEW WORKER ELITE

The increasing prevalence of wives employed full time — and the concomitant maintenance of income — does not represent a surcease of demands on husbands similarly to be full-time employees. While nearly half of all married-couple families had wives in the labor force in 1979, only 19.3 percent had both the husband and the wife working year round full time (Exhibit 44), though up sharply from 15.6 percent in 1975. This "dual-income" pattern is most accentuated in the 25 to 44 years of age sector — into which the baby-boom generation will fully shift by the late 1980s. While this may represent a very substantial reservoir of potential income additions, whether such shifts portend real income growth, or conversely, at best serve to prevent real income deterioration, is open to very real question. Certainly the addition of almost two million dual-income married couples (both working full time, year round), only permitted overall family income stabilization in the later stages of the 1970s.

The income levels attendant to the new worker elite are shown in Exhibit 45. Not only are there income "premiums" accompanying husband-wife full-time

* The 1979 data are the latest available tabulations detailing employment status of wives and mulitiple worker families.

EXHIBIT 44

All Husband-Wife (Married Couple) Families and Husband and Wife Both Year-Round Full Time Workers: 1975 and 1979

(Numbers in Thousands)

	1975			1979		
Age of Wife	**All Husband-Wife Wife Families**	**Husband & Wife Year-Round Full-time Workers**		**All Married Couple Families**	**Husband-Wife Both Year-Round Full-time Workers**	
		Number	**Percent**		**Number**	**Percent**
Total	47,318[1]	7,385	15.6%	48,180[1]	9,308	19.3%
Wife 14-24 years	5,381	800	14.9	4,825[2]	926	19.2
25-44 years	20,966	3,781	18.0	22,059	5,407	24.5
45-64 years	13,365	2,760	16.9	16,046	2,934	18.3

Notes: [1]Includes wife 65 years of age and over.
[2]15 to 24 years.

Source: U.S. Bureau of the Census, Current Population Reports, Series P-60, No. 105, *Money Income in 1975 of Families and Persons in the United States,* U.S. Government Printing Office, Washington, D.C., 1977.
1979 Data, U.S. Bureau of the Census, Advance of Publication.

EXHIBIT 45

Median Family Incomes, All Husband-Wife (Married Couple) Families and Householder (Head) Year-Round Full-Time Worker with Wife Employed Full Time: 1975 and 1979[1]

	All Married Couples (Husband-Wife) Families				Householder (Head) Year-Round Full-Time Worker, Wife Employed Full-Time			
			Change 1975 to 1979				Change: 1975 to 1979	
	1975	1979	Number	Percent	1975	1979	Number	Percent
Total	$14,867	$21,503	$6,636	44.6%	$20,185	$28,189	$8,004	39.7%
Householder (Head)								
(14) 15-24 years[2]	9,916	16,880	6,964	70.2	14,292	20,048	5,756	40.3
25-34	14,821	21,296	6,475	43.7	18,510	25,575	7,065	38.2
35-44	17,343	25,424	8,081	46.6	21,318	29,627	8,309	39.0
45-54	18,823	27,542	8,719	46.3	23,160	32,559	9,399	40.6
55-64	15,553	23,028	7,475	48.1	21,693	30,742	9,049	41.7

Notes: [1]Labels in parenthesis refer to 1975 definition.
[2]14 years in 1975; 15 years in 1979.

Source: U.S. Bureau of the Census, Current Population Reports, Series P-60, No. 105, *Money Income in 1975 of Families and Persons in the United States,* U.S. Government Printing Office, Washington, D.C., 1977.
1979 Data, U.S. Bureau of the Census, Advance of Publication.

employment status ($28,189) — versus all married-couple families ($21,503) — there is also a "bonus" as a function of age. The elite in terms of 1979 median income of all the groups shown in Exhibit 45 are married-couple families whose head is between 45 and 54 years of age — and in which both principals are employed full time year round. The households that meet these requirements have incomes in excess of $32,000 per year. Above and below that age group incomes are significantly lower.

It is striking to note that with the exception of very youthful households, i.e., the small group with householders 24 years of age or under, it is the more mature groups who have shown the greatest absolute and percentage income growth. This holds true whether one takes all married couples as a set or simply the multiple-full-time-worker elites.

It is this demographic-age-related income premium which has been readily embraced as a portent of brighter market opportunities to come — of a maturing baby boom of increased productivity and work experience flush with disposable income. But in a world economy of increasingly furious competition, the 1980s may be hard put to replicate the limited achievements of the 1970s.

SUMMARY

Despite shifts of great magnitude between 1975 and 1979 in the working patterns of American families — of nearly 2 million more married couples with both spouses working year round full time — of over 3 million additional working wives — the median family incomes of American families in constant dollars have remained relatively immutable.

1. Since 1973, the median family income in the United States declined by $1,300, from $22,346 (in constant 1980 dollars) in 1973 to $21,023 in 1980.
2. This pattern occurred even with the addition of far more dual-income families than single-spouse families.
3. Despite adding a new multiple-worker "elite," the absolute number of families with incomes $25,000 a year and over has barely expanded over the decade — its proportion to total families indeed has declined. The number of hours of gainful employment required of the principals in American families in order to maintain their income levels has expanded enormously.
4. The aggregate results in terms of overall family affluence barely seems to have been affected. The casual beliefs that the demographics of the 1980s will in themselves generate a new boom are belied by the lid of the post-1973 economy. The impact of these new dynamics in terms of consumption patterns — and the conventional wisdom — will be reviewed in the following chapter.

Chapter Eight

THE BABY BOOM AND CONSUMPTION

The 1970s marked the abrupt termination of the historic post-World War II pattern of sustained real family-income gains. But this topping out was countered by an increase in the nominal personal capital of a majority of American families, reflected in the inflated values of their built-up housing equity. This "paper" security permitted and encouraged a pattern of decline in real savings, thereby facilitating the continued expansion of personal consumption expenditures (chapter 6). The economy of the 1970s was unabashedly consumer-led.

Its cutting edge was the baby-boom generation, which created burgeoning markets at each of its life-cycle stages. Out of this experience — our litany usually extends from diapers in the 1950s, soft drinks and teen-rock in the 1960s to labeled blue jeans and stereos in the 1970s — evolved the major thesis of current demographic-oriented business forecasting: riding the baby boom through its various life-cycle changes is the clear prescription for success.

The early part of the decade of the 1970s had a variety of institutional triumphs that were very clear-cut exemplars of this format. Prime among them were youth-oriented national specialty-apparel chain stores, whose vitality and growth power throughout the decade far outpaced their more diversified conventional peers — the department stores. Epitomizing such operations was the proliferation of "The Gap" stores and equivalent purveyors to the then teeny-bopper generation and later to their maturing derrieres. Equally compelling to the conventional wisdom of life-cycle "riding" is the experience of other chains in this category: Casual Corner, Petrie Stores, Limited Stores, Lerner Shops, Brooks Fashion Stores, and Miller-Wohl.

It is interesting to note in this context that this success had other demographic underpinnings. Most of the major national chains engaged in specialty retailing grew concurrently with the advent of regional shopping centers, which both foresaw and reflected general suburban population dominance (chapter 12). The synergism of suburban population shifts, the rise of large-scale regional malls and the emergence of the latter as the focal points of the youth generation — which undoubtedly led to the fiscal vigor of the specialty store business — radically altered the retailing landscape of America.

LIFE-CYCLE ANALYSIS AND THE MAGIC BULLET

But too much can be ascribed to this same eruption of fecundity. For example, many of the shortcomings of the American economy in the 1970s, from the lack of productivity, i.e., the feckless worker, to the failure to save, have been ascribed to the massive influx of inexperienced baby boomers into their first low-paying jobs and the rapid proliferation of single-person households (as suggested in chapter 6). And conversely, as we view the 1980s, the espoused wisdom is of a maturing, increasingly productive baby-boom cohort, configured into two earner households, which will generate in their train all of the building blocks of reindustrialization and a vibrant consumer economy.

But to quote Gershwin, "It ain't necessarily so." The problems of forecasting require not merely a mechanistic view of the conventional wisdom of personal behavior and consumption patterns, but also cognizance of the constraints of a faltering national economy immersed in an increasingly competitive world environment — and a government which must face up to the realities of the midlife crisis of the American capitalist system.

PRECEDENT

The very concept of the baby boom has had at least two different definitions. Predicated on a fertility rate threshold of 3.0 first achieved in 1947, the leading edge of the baby-boom generation would have been a relatively mature 29 years of age in 1976 — 33 years by 1980. (The baby-boom delineation in chapter 2 is based on directional changes — a sharp upward surge in 1946 and a peaking in 1957.) By the definition of quanta, i.e., 4.0 million births or more per year, first achieved in 1954, the equivalent figures would have been 22 years of age in 1976 and 26 years by 1980. By either definition, the fabled demographic bulge matured within this four year period so that its own personal income resources could be brought to bear on the nation's consumption patterns. (Previous life-cycle marketing successes were largely predicated on the continually replenished parental purse, during the rise to affluence in the post-World War II, pre-oil-embargo decades.)

However, as we review the shifts in very broad classifications of expenditures from 1976 to 1980, there is little of the conventional wisdom of a baby-boom-led surge reflected in them. As presented in Exhibit 46, there were only three exceptional growth sectors in that four-year period: housing, medical care, and personal business. This contrasted sharply with the five

EXHIBIT 46
Personal Consumption Expenditures by Type of Expenditure: 1976 and 1980
(Billions of Current Dollars)

			Change: 1976-1980	
	1976	**1980**	**Number**	**Percent**
TOTAL CONSUMPTION	$1,084.3	$1,672.8	$588.5	54.3%
Food and Tobacco	247.0	366.1	119.1	48.2
Clothing, Accessories and Jewelry	88.6	123.5	34.9	39.3
Personal Care	15.6	23.3	7.7	49.4
Housing	166.5	272.0	105.5	63.4
Household Operation	148.3	228.9	80.6	54.3
Medical Care	98.4	166.0	67.6	68.7
Personal Business	55.6	90.8	35.2	63.3
Transportation	155.2	243.0	87.8	56.6
Recreation	72.5	106.4	33.9	46.8
Other	36.6	52.7	16.1	44.0

Source: U.S. Department of Commerce, Bureau of Economic Analysis, *Survey of Current Business,* Volume 61, No. 7, July 1981; and Special Supplement, *Survey of Current Business,* National Income and Product Accounts, 1976-79, July 1981.

lagging sectors of food and tobacco, clothing, accessories and jewelry, personal care, recreation (remember all of the hoopla about recreation?), and the catchall "other." Household operations and transportation remained essentially constant in market share, i.e., grew at a rate comparable to that demonstrated by overall consumption.

Further examination of the 107 more detailed — but still relatively broad — expenditure partitions provided in the National Income and Product Accounts offers only limited additional clarification of the above pattern. Excepting only medical care and personal business, increases in personal consumption were dominated by housing, housing-related energy, and transportation-related energy costs. Certainly, the latter elements served as effective caps in constraining uniquely demographic inspired expenditures.

Moreover, personal consumption was also impacted by shifts in personal savings. Total consumption expenditures from 1976 to 1980 increased by more than half (Exhibit 46), from $1.08 trillion to $1.67 trillion. The savings rates which accompanied this splurge plunged from a level approaching 8 percent at the beginning of 1976 to a meager 5 percent in 1980.

THE CLASH BETWEEN THE BULLS AND BEARS OF SUPPLY AND DEMAND

Principal among the emerging parameters of government policy which will either increase or decrease the flow of consumer expenditures are the proposed levels of personal tax decreases. And certainly these will provide a significant positive impetus in potentially deepening the consumer's pocket. Countering them, however, may well be the issue of preferences for savings versus consumption.

The pattern of "Spend and borrow now, tomorrow the dollar will be lighter," has become intolerable to all parties. Thus that part of the consumption spree fueled by the inflationary surge will be reduced. In addition, while the clash of rival economic theories on the detrimental role and impact of government deficits has not been resolved at this writing, withal there is a general consensus which acknowledges the necessity for encouraging more in the way of personal savings, of making the holding of dollars competitive with the collection of beer cans, stamps, diamonds, gold — and perhaps even of housing. (In these heady days of money-market funds fluctuating between 10 and 20 percent, one should not lose sight of the fact that the 1970s were characterized by the virtual impossibility of securing a positive post-tax, post-inflation real rate of return on savings. The 5½ percent passbook account will soon be a curious historical artifact.)

The full impact of formal tax incentives to saving, such as the capacity to reinvest dividends tax-free in select electrical utilities, the All-Savers Certificates and the new IRA accounts, powerful though they may be, could be of less significance than the long-sought-for retreat from inflationary expectation. Regardless of their rival vigors, the combination of alternatives to spending are formidable.

And these are just the positive inhibitors to the immediate flourishing of the market. To them, on a far less constructive note, may well be added the levels of economic uncertainty and of relatively high, sticky unemployment which seem to address the economy with sickening regularity. The calculus of selected boom consumption expenditures based on demography must meet the challenge of macro-economic reality.

THE TRANSPORTATION ALLEGORY

The forecaster is the child of history masquerading as seer. A case in point, which may have broader ramifications as we enter the uncertainties of the 1980s, is the area of transportation (Exhibit 47). New-automobile expenditures increased by a paltry 21.6 percent from 1976 to 1980. When inflation is factored in, the dollar increment from \$38 billion in the base year to \$46 billion at the terminal point is a sad paraphrase of the decline of Detroit.

The complement to new-automobile personal expenditures is the personal-

EXHIBIT 47
Personal Consumption Expenditures: Transportation and Major Components
(Billions of Current Dollars)

	1976	1980	Change: 1976-1980 Number	Percent
TRANSPORTATION	$155.2	$243.0	$87.8	56.6%
User Operated Transportation	144.1	224.3	80.2	55.7
New Automobiles	*38.0*	*46.2*	*8.2*	*21.6*
Gasoline and Oil	*43.9*	*89.0*	*45.1*	*102.7*
Repair, Parking & Rental	21.3	34.4	13.1	61.5
Insurance Premiums	5.4	10.0	4.6	85.2
Purchased Local Transportation	4.4	6.1	1.7	38.6
Purchased Intercity Transportation	6.7	12.7	6.0	89.6

New Automobile Expenditures

1976	$38.1
1977	44.5
1978	48.3
1979	49.4
1980	46.2

Source: U.S. Department of Commerce, Bureau of Economic Analysis, *Survey of Current Business,* Volume 61, No. 7, July 1981; and Special Supplement, *Survey of Current Business,* National Income and Product Accounts, 1976-79, July 1981.

transportation consumption of gasoline and oil, which more than doubled (102.7 percent) over the same time frame. Indeed, if we were to group the two together, they would yield a very respectable 65-percent increase, well above those of transportation generally or indeed for all consumer expenditures. But in 1976 expenditures on new automobiles and gasoline and oil were roughly comparable ($38.0 billion versus $43.9 billion). By 1980, the former was but half the latter ($46.2 billion versus $89.0 billion).

What we have had very simply is an enormous transfer of the receipts of consumer spending on transportation from the industrial heartland of America, i.e., car manufacturing, to the oil producers and refiners of the world. The rise of Houston and the crumbling of Detroit are complementary.

Yet the cutting edge of the baby boom, by historic definition, should have been entering into the peak of first-time car ownership at the same time automobile producers were entering into their decline. At the beginning of this period, Ford was bemoaning a physical plant that could turn out "only" 5 million cars a year. By the end of this period of nominal demographic glory, it was sharply chopping back its scale of operations. Yet the decline in absolute automobile registration which has been noted in a number of states is viewed not as an inkling of things to come but rather an indication of a dammed-up well of consumer demand. The president of General Motors has predicted a 12-million-car-sale year as just around the corner. Fortunately, for forecasters, audiences seldom have a knowledge of history.

The noise of external events may very well overwhelm the signals of population profiles. The rise of the world economy has not been met with an equivalent development of forecasting technique. The latter at best was always far from perfect — it is now fraught with increasing risks and uncertainty. The segmentation of markets will become ever more demanding and complex as the 1980s unfold.

SEGMENTATION AND ECONOMIC CONSTRAINTS

The vast, monolithic middle-class market that dominated the United States economy began to fragment during the 1970s. The struggle to "catchup" and adapt is now visible on all fronts. The shopping-center industry has run out of large-scale untapped markets and now must recognize and reflect diversity and market segmentation. And the housing industry, too, is mired in the malaise that emanates from the intersection of economic events and demographic trends — and a failure to generate new products.

The segmentation of baby boom households into single-and dual-income formats is well recognized. But given the constraints and limitations noted earlier, much more extensive partitioning will be required to isolate truly "upscale" market segments. One dimension of powerful significance may be the housing "train."

At this writing, it is almost shocking to recall that it was still possible to secure long-term fixed-interest-rate mortgages between 8 and 9 percent as late as 1978. Those who boarded the housing train at or before that time may be better able to weather broader economic constraints than their younger and less fortunate peers. The later stages of the baby-boom generation may well be saddled permanently with a web of housing costs that can severely retard discretionary spending for the forseeable future. Denied a seat on the housing train, this younger cohort could conceivably be relegated to a market position far below what its sheer size should portend.

SUMMARY

The fortunes of a life-cycle rider may be particularly hazardous in the 1980s. The whole gives every incidence of being *less* than the sum of its parts. Refined and defined market segmentation rather than broad trend analysis will be required. Casual acceptance of the belief in a massive maturing baby-boom consumption spree to come may lead to consequences similar to those now being borne by Detroit.

1. A myriad of retailing successes of the past generation was predicated on the burgeoning markets created by each of the life-cycle stages of the baby-boom generation, leading to a major thesis of current demographic-oriented business forecasting: riding the baby boom through the various life-cycle changes as the clear prescription for success.
2. But the lid on the national economy (chapter 6) and its constraining effects on income (chapter 7) raise severe challenges to the recent conventional wisdom.
3. During the late 1970s (1976 to 1980), when the maturing baby boom nominally should have brought its own personal income resources to bear on the nation's consumption patterns, there was little evidence of a unique baby-boom-led surge within them.
4. Dominating the increases in personal consumption were housing, housing-related energy, and transportation-related energy expenditures, which served as effective caps in constraining uniquely demographic-occasioned expenditures.
5. Moreover, even this consumption was facilitated by a decline in the savings rate from 8 percent in 1976 to below 5 percent during 1980. The government-inspired encouragement of personal savings during the 1980s — in order to secure more vigorous capital investment — may act as a consumption inhibitor as the decade evolves.
6. Clearly, the calculus of selected boom consumption expenditures based on demography must meet the challenge of macroeconomic reality.
7. Transportation may stand as a harbinger of history to come. In 1976, expenditures on new automobiles and gasoline and oil (for personal transportation) were roughly comparable ($38.0 billion versus $43.9 billion). By 1980, the former ($46.2 billion) was but half the latter ($89.0 billion), leaving Detroit gasping in its wake.
8. Thus we have had an enormous transfer of the receipts of transportation consumer spending from car manufacturing to the oil producers and refiners of the world — and this at a time when expected baby-boom new-car purchases should have set a furious pace.
9. Does this experience foreshadow the impending struggle of demographic and economic reality over the decade of the 1980s? An affirmative answer is strongly warranted, particularly as housing and its demographic-related foundations are examined. It is to this linkage which we now shift.

Chapter Nine

DEMOGRAPHICS AND HOUSING

The linkage between demographic reality and the availability, cost, and configuration of shelter is of major significance to the economy as well as to American folkway. The emphasis of this chapter is on the dynamism of the interrelationship, i.e., while demographics typically are viewed as the inspiration for housing demand, in part the reverse also holds true — the availability of housing of various configurations clearly has a significant impact on demographic parameters: rates of household formation, birth, divorce, and labor-force participation.

From the viewpoint of public policy, equally important dimensions revolve around the issues of whether housing investment displaced other forms of saving or resources for productive activity. The decision on the national level to remove housing finance from the unique institutional and cost umbrella which had evolved since the early days of the New Deal signals a basic change in the market. The full implications of this phenomenon are not adequately understood. For example, though there are many locomotives to the American economy, the housing cycle is as significant as any.

As demographers and economists viewed the 1980s, principal among the "assured" sectors of growth was housing. While some hesitation was expressed about the latter part of the decade, based upon the baby-bust generation entering the housing stream, there was remarkably little forecaster reluctance relating the maturing baby boom cohort to the powerhouse drive toward upgraded housing demands. Estimates of construction in excess of 25 million units were common.

In the analyses that follow, we have attempted to assemble a baseline linkage between housing and demography, viewing the latter not only in terms of gross numbers, but also in terms of market penetration by the various age/income/configurational attributes of households. In turn, these data reflect most strenuously on the *effective* demand that will be realized in the 1980s.

EXHIBIT 48

Changes in the Housing Inventory, U.S. Total: 1960, 1970 and 1980

(Numbers in Thousands)

				Change: 1960-1970		Change: 1970-1980	
	1960	1970	1980	Number	Percent	Number	Percent
All Housing Units	58,326	68,672	88,397	10,346	17.7	19,725	28.7
Year-Round Units	56,584	67,699	86,678	11,115	19.6	18,979	28.0
Occupied Units	53,024	63,445	80,378	10,421	19.7	16,933	26.7
Owner Occupied	32,797	39,886	51,787	7,089	21.6	11,901	29.8
Percent of Total	61.9	62.9	64.4	—	—	—	—
Renter Occupied	20,227	23,560	28,591	3,333	16.5	5,031	21.4
Percent of Total	38.1	37.1	35.6	—	—	—	—

Source: U.S. Department of Commerce, Bureau of the Census, *Census of Population and Housing 1960, 1970 and 1980.*

THE GLORIOUS DECADE

The 1970s in retrospect were the years of triumph for the American housing delivery system. The net increase in housing units between 1970 and 1980 came close to the 20-million-unit level (Exhibit 48). While precise data on demolitions and conversions — phenomena that removed substantial numbers of housing units from the market — are not available at this writing, the best estimates would indicate that the net increase (19.7 million units) over the decade was generated by gross additions on the order of 25 to 26 million housing units. The contrast with the decade of the 1960s, frequently viewed as one of more vigorous general growth, is particularly telling. The 1970s generated nearly twice as many housing units as the 1960s, with both owner and rental units flourishing nearly on a par.

This success was achieved despite enormous variations in the level of annual housing starts (Exhibit 49). The rollercoaster ride of 2 million privately owned

EXHIBIT 49

New Privately Owned Housing Started, By Structure Size, United States Total: 1964 to 1980

(Numbers in Thousands)

			In Structures With					
	Total		1 Unit		2 to 4 Units		5 Units or More	
Year	Number	Percent	Number	Percent	Number	Percent	Number	Percent
1964	1,529	100.0	971	63.5	108	7.1	450	29.4
1965	1,473	100.0	964	65.4	87	5.9	422	28.6
1966	1,165	100.0	779	66.9	61	5.2	325	27.9
1967	1,292	100.0	844	65.3	72	5.6	376	29.1
1968	1,508	100.0	899	59.6	82	5.4	527	34.9
1969	1,467	100.0	811	55.3	85	5.8	571	38.9
1970	1,434	100.0	813	56.7	85	5.9	536	37.4
1971	2,052	100.0	1,151	56.1	120	5.8	781	38.1
1972	2,356	100.0	1,309	55.6	141	6.0	906	38.5
1973	2,045	100.0	1,132	55.4	118	5.8	795	38.9
1974	1,338	100.0	888	66.4	68	5.1	382	28.6
1975	1,160	100.0	892	76.9	64	5.5	204	17.6
1976	1,538	100.0	1,162	75.5	87	5.7	289	18.8
1977	1,987	100.0	1,451	73.0	122	6.1	414	20.8
1978	2,020	100.0	1,433	70.9	125	6.2	462	22.9
1979	1,745	100.0	1,194	68.4	122	7.0	429	24.6
1980	1,292	100.0	852	65.9	109	8.4	331	25.6

Note: Numbers and percents may not add due to rounding.

Source U.S. Bureau of Census, Department of Commerce, *Construction Reports*, "Housing Starts," C20 (Washington, D.C.: U.S. Government Printing Office, Monthly).

housing-unit starts in one year, followed by annual levels barely half that figure, with subsequent years then again broaching the 2-million-unit heights, characterized the decade. Housing performed one of its significant macroeconomic roles: that of a stabilizing countercyclical element. Government-encouraged housing programs were pumped in at times of recession while there was practically an automatic stabilizer in withdrawal of funds from the market for other, higher-paying purposes when the economy overheated.

The major shifts in consumer preference as expressed in rival consumption patterns between renting and homeownership reviewed below were a tribute to the enabling capacity of cheap, long-term money in the face of inflation. The virtual disappearance of the latter will alter our shelter patterns. Changes in this order that are currently attending the homogenization of financial markets are monumental in their impact and—short of major federal policy shifts — irreversible.[19]

THE DEMOGRAPHICS OF MARKET PENETRATION

The trends toward increasing homeownership in America certainly extend back not only to the end of World War II, but to the pre-depression era. The dominance of ownership that had been achieved in the 1950s and 1960s was strikingly confirmed and, if anything, accentuated in terms of variance in market penetration by household configurations and income class in the 1970s. Some insight into the pervasiveness of the phenomenon is provided in Exhibits 50, 51 and 52, which define owner and renter households by composition and by age of head.

As Exhibit 50 indicates, renter occupied facilities increasingly became the domain of the non-modular households, with reductions in every one of the age subconfigurations of male head-wife present (married couple) families. Indeed, for the latter group as a whole, the absolute loss is particularly striking. While the total number of renter households increased by 15.3-percent, male-headed, wife-present formats declined by more than a fifth (-21 percent). The sectors of most vigorous rental growth were the "atypical" household configurations.

The absolute increase in homeownership in all household categories (Exhibit 51) obscures some of the internal dynamics which were taking place. There is striking penetration of homeownership into household configurations that were long thought to be outside this domain. This phenomenon is further clarified in Exhibit 52. The abrupt withdrawal of husband-wife families from rental facilities is strikingly pronounced, as is the near comparable growth in homeownership for non-modular households. Even in single-person households, the rate of increase in ownership outpaced its rental equivalent.

EXHIBIT 50

Renter-Occupied Units, Household Composition by Age of Head 1970 and 1979

(Numbers in Thousands)

Household Composition by Age of Head	1970	1979	Change: 1970-1979 Number	Percent
Total Renter Occupied	23,560	27,160	3,600	15.3
2-or-More Person Households	17,171	17,412	241	1.4
Male Head, Wife Present	12,759	10,063	2,696	-21.1
Under 25 years	2,282	1,702	-580	-25.4
25 to 29 Years	2,408	2,166	-242	-10.0
30 to 34 Years	1,531	1,461	-70	-4.6
35 to 44 Years	2,154	1,628	-526	-24.4
45 to 64 Years	3,148	2,019	-1,129	-35.9
65 Years and Over	1,236	1,087	-149	-12.1
Other Male Head	1,143	2,090	947	82.9
Under 65 Years	1,010	1,995	985	97.5
65 Years and Over	132	95	-37	-28.0
Female Head	3,270	5,259	1,989	60.8
Under 65 Years	2,899	4,868	1,969	67.9
65 Years and Over	370	391	21	5.7
1-Person Households	6,389	9,748	3,359	52.6
Under 65 Years	4,109	6,716	2,607	63.4
65 Years and Over	2,279	3,032	753	33.0

Note: Numbers may not add due to rounding.

Source: U.S. Department of Commerce, Bureau of the Census, *Current Housing Reports,* Series H-150-79, *Annual Housing Survey: 1979, Parts A and C.* U.S. Government Printing Office, Washington, D.C., 1981.

INCOME LINKAGES

In preceding chapters we have detailed income variations as a function of household configuration. So important are these elements, however, to household shelter/tenure relationships as to make them worthy of restatement. In Exhibit 53 are shown owner and renter household incomes by household configuration. The far-right column indicates the ratio of renter to

EXHIBIT 51
Owner-Occupied Units, Household Composition by Age of Head 1970 and 1979
(Numbers in Thousands)

Household Composition by Age of Head	1970	1979	Change: 1970-1979 Number	Change: 1970-1979 Percent
Total Owner Occupied	39,886	51,411	11,525	28.9
2-or-More Person Households	35,124	43,424	8,300	23.6
Male Head, Wife Present	30,806	37,058	6,252	20.3
Under 25 years	800	1,018	218	27.3
25 to 29 Years	2,252	3,106	854	37.9
30 to 34 Years	2,938	4,409	1,471	50.1
35 to 44 Years	7,097	8,066	969	13.7
45 to 64 Years	13,230	14,540	1,310	9.9
65 Years and Over	4,490	5,919	1,429	31.8
Other Male Head	1,298	1,932	634	48.8
Under 65 Years	974	1,581	607	62.3
65 Years and Over	324	351	27	8.3
Female Head	3,019	4,435	1,416	46.9
Under 65 Years	2,159	3,398	1,239	57.4
65 Years and Over	860	1,037	177	20.6
1-Person Households	4,762	7,987	3,225	67.7
Under 65 Years	2,075	3,685	1,610	77.6
65 Years and Over	2,688	4,302	1,614	60.0

Source: U.S. Department of Commerce, Bureau of the Census, *Current Housing Reports,* Series H-150-79, *Annual Housing Survey: 1979, Parts A and C.* U.S. Government Printing Office, Washington, D.C., 1981.

owner income. As is evident from the data, renters generally have much less in the way of fiscal resource than is available to their owner peers (stabilizing for household configuration). The most competitive renter households (male-head, wife-present formats), i.e., having the highest income ratio to their owner equivalents, are just the group who have been leaving rental facilities.

And these are relationships that deteriorated over time (Exhibit 54), i.e., as the decade matured, the divergence between owner and renter incomes was magnified. Those with adequate resources increasingly tended to move into home-ownership; rental facilities increasingly were the province of the financially poor. The economic class linkage to homeownership referred to in earlier chapters is clearly defined in the trends.

EXHIBIT 52

Owner and Renter Households, Change in Composition by Age of Head: 1970-1979

(Percentage Change)

Household Composition By Age of Head	Renter	Owner
Total Households	15.3%	28.9%
2-or-More Person Households	1.4	23.6
Male Head, Wife Present	-21.1	20.3
Under 25 Years	-25.4	27.3
25 to 29 Years	-10.0	37.9
30 to 34 Years	-4.6	50.1
35 to 44 Years	-24.4	13.7
45 to 64 Years	-35.9	9.9
65 Years and Over	-12.1	31.8
Other Male Head	82.9	48.8
Under 65 Years	97.5	62.3
65 Years and Over	-28.0	8.3
Female Head	60.8	46.9
Under 65 Years	67.9	57.4
65 Years and Over	5.7	20.6
1-Person Households	52.6	67.7
Under 65 Years	63.4	77.6
65 Years and Over	33.0	60.0

Source: U.S. Department of Commerce, Bureau of the Census, *Current Housing Reports,* Series H-150-79, *Annual Housing Survey: 1979, Parts A and C.* U.S. Government Printing Office, Washington, D.C., 1981.

SHELTER COST PARAMETERS

The stagnation of real incomes defined in chapter 7 is the result of inflated incomes failing to keep pace with an equally inflated consumer-price index. The latter, however, tends to obscure some of the important variations attached to individual cost components. In Exhibit 55 are presented some data pertinent to shelter costs. While the overall CPI (all items) increased by less than a third (31.1 percent) from 1960 to 1970, the level of increment nearly quadrupled (112.4 percent) in the decade of the 1970s. There is a very clear-cut

EXHIBIT 53
Owner and Renter Household Income
By Household Configuration
U.S. Total: 1979

Household Composition By Age of Head	Total Owner Occupied	Total Renter Occupied	Renter/ Owner Ratio
Total Households	$18,400	$10,000	.54
2-or-More Person Households	20,400	11,600	.57
Male Head, Wife Present	21,600	14,200	.66
Under 25 years	15,900	12,500	.79
25 to 29 Years	20,600	15,200	.74
30 to 34 Years	22,700	15,900	.70
35 to 44 Years	24,600	16,400	.67
45 to 64 Years	23,900	15,000	.63
65 Years and Over	11,100	8,800	.79
Other Male Head	17,800	10,800	.61
Under 65 Years	19,200	11,000	.57
65 Years and Over	11,600	6,900	.59
Female Head	12,400	7,000	.56
Under 65 Years	13,000	6,900	.53
65 Years and Over	10,300	7,000	.68
1-Person Households	7,200	7,500	1.04
Under 65 Years	11,800	9,800	.83
65 Years and Over	5,600	4,700	.84

Source: U.S. Department of Commerce, Bureau of the Census, *Current Housing Reports,* Series H-150-79, *Annual Housing Survey: 1979, Parts A and C.* U.S. Government Printing Office, Washington, D.C., 1981.

acceleration, as the data are reviewed, in five—year intervals, increasing steadily from 6.5 percent (1960 to 1965) to 53.2 percent (1975 to 1980). Homeownership-related costs moved even more rapidly than the CPI as a whole. This was partially a function of energy-cost hikes, indicated in Exhibit 55, as well as the composite of mortgage-interest rates and soaring housing-price levels (which are detailed later in this chapter).

Rents actually lagged behind the CPI, with increments typically staying under two-thirds of those of the broader measurement. The controversy over whether the failure of renter incomes or, conversely, the failure of rental facilities to attract higher-income individuals, accounts for this moderation —

EXHIBIT 54
Trends in Renter/Owner Income Ratios: 1973, 1976 and 1979

Household Composition By Age of Head	Renter/Owner Income Ratios 1973	1976	1979
Total Households	.63	.56	.54
2-or-More Person Households	.68	.60	.57
Male Head, Wife Present	.73	.69	.66
Under 25 years	.85	.77	.79
25 to 29 Years	.83	.78	.74
30 to 34 Years	.77	.73	.70
35 to 44 Years	.72	.67	.67
45 to 64 Years	.74	.68	.63
65 Years and Over	.80	.79	.79
Other Male Head	.69	.59	.61
Under 65 Years	.66	.54	.57
65 Years and Oveer	.65	.67	.59
Female Head	.73	.62	.56
Under 65 Years	.68	.59	.53
65 Years and Over	.75	.72	.68
1 Person Households	1.13	1.08	1.04
Under 65 Years	.98	.91	.83
65 Years and Over	—	.81	.84

Source: U.S. Department of Commerce, Bureau of the Census, *Current Housing Reports,* Series H-150-79, *Annual Housing Survey: 1979, Parts A and C.* U.S. Government Printing Office, Washington, D.C., 1981; and *Annual Housing Survey,* 1973 and 1976.

or whether this largely resulted from the poor staying within the relatively modestly inflated sanctuary of rental facilities — while the affluent benefited from post-inflation homeownership shelter costs are very basic issues as we view the past and attempt to predict the future. Regardless of the weight of the factors that are at work, it is clear that homeownership secured striking increases in market penetration despite its soaring threshold costs.

As detailed in chapters 7 and 8, the shift from housing as shelter to housing as refuge from inflation, and increasingly as a speculative device, made it possible for the market to surmount the impediments to home acquisition. The latter are detailed in Exhibits 56 and 57, which show the evolution of

EXHIBIT 55

Consumer Price Index, United States, Selected Items: 1960 to 1980

Year	All Items	Home Ownership	Rent	Fuel Oil and Coal	Gas and Electricity
1960	88.7	86.3	91.7	89.2	98.6
1965	94.5	92.7	96.9	94.6	99.4
1970	116.3	128.5	110.1	110.1	107.3
1971	121.3	133.7	115.2	117.5	114.7
1972	125.3	140.1	119.2	118.5	120.5
1973	133.1	146.7	124.3	136.0	126.4
1974	147.7	163.2	130.6	214.6	145.8
1975	161.2	181.7	137.3	235.3	169.6
1976	170.5	191.7	144.7	250.8	189.0
1977	181.5	204.9	153.5	283.4	213.4
1978	195.4	227.2	164.0	298.3	232.6
1979	217.7	263.6	175.9	403.6	257.9
1980	247.0	314.0	191.6	556.0	301.8
		Percentage Change			
Period					
1960-1970	31.1	48.9	20.1	23.4	8.8
1960-1965	6.5	7.4	5.7	6.1	0.8
1965-1970	23.1	38.6	13.6	16.4	7.9
1970-1975	38.6	41.4	24.7	113.7	58.1
1975-1980	53.2	72.8	39.5	136.3	77.9
1970-1980	112.4	144.4	74.0	405.0	181.3

Note: 1970 to 1979 — Wage Earners and Clerical Workers (CPI-W)
1980 — All Urban Consumers (CPI-U)

Source Bureau of Economic Analysis, U.S. Department of Commerce, *Survey of Current Business* (Washington, D.C.: U.S. Government Printing Office, Annual.

home-mortgage loan rates as well as median sales prices.

As we review the closing years of the 1970s, the capacity of housing starts to withstand the enormous, unprecedented increases in effective interest rates detailed in Exhibit 56 clearly was a unique phenomenon. Much more modest cost increments historically had been viewed as basically "turning off the faucet of housing" yet housing demand and, as shown in Exhibit 57, housing-price surges, seemed capable of withstanding the ever greater fiscal burdens placed upon homeowners.

In our opinion, the current housing scene suffers from enlarged volumes of housing purchases and construction resulting from the housing-buying panic

EXHIBIT 56
Conventional Home Mortgage Loan Rates,
25-Year Maturity: National Averages For All Major Types of Lenders[1]

Year	Loan to Price Ratio					
	Contract Interest Rate			Effective Interest Rate[2]		
	50%	75%	90%	50%	75%	90%
1977	8.71	8.79	9.01	8.88	8.96	9.22
1978	9.43	9.50	9.69	9.63	9.69	9.95
1979	10.94	11.00	11.23	11.20	11.27	11.54
1980	13.60	13.63	13.80	13.97	14.00	14.21
April 1981	15.07	15.10	15.28	15.50	15.53	15.75
September 1981	17.23	17.26	17.40	17.73	17.77	17.95

Notes: [1]Savings and loan associations, mortgage bankers, commercial banks, and mutual savings banks.
[2]Contract rate plus initial fees and charges amortized over 10 years.

Source: Federal Home Loan Bank Board, *The Federal Home Loan Bank Board Journal,* Monthly.

that characterized the last years of the decade. Thus in a sense we have borrowed housing starts from the future.[20]

Again retrospective analysis provides some measure of chastening warning as we view in Exhibit 57 the relative slowdown in the median sales prices of new one-family houses sold in the United States. Housing prices, when viewed in the context of overall levels of inflation, clearly are being braked.[21] But certainly the decade long pattern was one of overwhelming increment.

The factors that lay behind regional variations in prices are considered in chapters 10 and 11. It is striking, however, to view the increasing homogenization of absolute price levels between the Northeast, North Central, and South regions, as well as the relative modest gains characteristic of the more mature sectors of the United States. And this is a pattern that is clearly replicated in the sales prices of existing single-family homes (Exhibit 58).

INCOME-SALES PRICE RELATIONSHIPS

There has been a long, if not inspired, debate on the issue of the relationship of the sales prices of new homes to median family incomes. Variations in base years are often used either to assert a degeneration in the capacity of Americans to buy new homes or to deny its validity. Certainly, however, in the last several years the ratios of sales price to income have been well over the 3.0 level while historically (in an era marked by far lower personal income taxes)

EXHIBIT 57

Median Sales Prices of New One Family Houses Sold: United States and Regions: 1963 to 1980

		Region			
Year	**United States**	**Northeast**	**North Central**	**South**	**West**
1963	$18,000	$20,300	$17,900	$16,100	$18,800
1964	18,900	20,300	19,400	16,700	20,400
1965	20,000	21,500	21,600	17,500	21,600
1966	21,400	23,500	23,200	18,200	23,200
1967	22,700	25,400	25,100	19,400	24,100
1968	24,700	27,700	27,400	21,500	25,100
1969	25,600	31,600	27,600	22,800	25,300
1970	23,400	30,300	24,400	20,300	24,000
1971	25,200	30,600	27,200	22,500	25,500
1972	27,600	31,400	29,300	25,800	27,500
1973	32,500	37,100	32,900	80,900	32,400
1974	35,900	40,100	36,100	34,500	35,800
1975	39,300	44,000	39,600	37,300	40,600
1976	44,200	47,300	44,800	40,500	47,200
1977	48,800	51,600	51,500	44,100	53,500
1978	55,700	58,100	59,200	50,300	61,300
1979	62,900	65,500	63,900	57,300	69,600
1980	64,500	69,300	63,300	59,700	72,300
		Percent Change			
1963 to 1970	30.0%	49.3%	36.3%	26.1%	27.7%
1970 to 1980	175.6	128.7	159.4	194.0	201.3

Source: U.S. Department of Commerce, Bureau of the Census, *Construction Reports,* "New One-Family Houses Sold and For Sale," Series C25 (Washington, D.C.: U.S. Government Printing Office, Monthly).

mortgage lenders have viewed more modest relationships as the appropriate measuring stick. Exhibit 59 indicates the substantial changes that have occurred over time.

It is important to emphasize that these gross relationships mask very important internal dynamics. Some of these are illustrated in Exhibit 60, which shows the linkage of demographically related median incomes to the median sales prices of new one-family homes. Even though there has been an increase in the income/share burden of home acquisition for all groups shown, this varies very substantially with household configuration and employment status. As late as 1979, the last year for which such detail is available, married-couple families with wives employed full time still fell

EXHIBIT 58

Median Sales Prices of Existing Single-Family Homes Sold, United States and Regions: 1970 to 1980

		Region			
Year	**United States**	**Northeast**	**North Central**	**South**	**West**
1970	$23,000	$25,200	$20,100	$22,200	$24,300
1971	24,800	27,100	22,100	24,300	26,500
1972	26,700	29,800	23,900	26,400	28,400
1973	28,900	32,800	25,300	29,000	31,000
1974	32,000	35,800	27,700	32,300	34,800
1975	35,300	39,300	30,100	34,800	39,600
1976	38,100	41,800	32,900	36,500	46,100
1977	42,900	44,400	36,700	39,800	57,300
1978	48,700	47,900	42,200	45,100	66,700
1979	55,700	53,600	47,800	51,300	77,400
1980	62,200	60,800	51,900	58,300	89,300
		Percent Change			
1970 to 1980	170.4%	141.3%	158.2%	162.6%	267.5%

Source: National Association of Realtors, *Existing Home Sales* (Washington, D.C.: Economics and Research Division, Monthly).

within the magic "two and a half times" ratio. Indeed, if both spouses were working year round full time, the ratio was still at the 2.2 level.

Even in these configurations of relative affluence, however, there are ominous signs of decay from 1975 to 1979. Regardless of household configuration, therefore, the relationship between median sales prices and median incomes clearly degenerated over time. And this cost-income problem is characteristic of renters as well.

RENT-INCOME RATIOS

Despite the comparative "bargain" of rental housing —its much more moderate level of increment than the CPI as a whole — gross rents as a percentage of income have moved up very forcefully. The data shown in Exhibit 61 illustrate the case. At the beginning of the 1970s, the median rent-income ratio stood at 20 percent. By the end of the decade the ratio soared over the "magic" 25 percent of income level. Thus by 1979, more than half of America's renters were paying in excess (26 percent) of the historic baseline of maximum acceptable shelter costs. It is particularly striking to note in Exhibit 6l the growing absolute number of American households

EXHIBIT 59

Median Sales Prices of New One-Family Houses Sold and Median Family Income, United States: 1954 to 1980

Year	Median Sales Price	Median Family Income	Ratio of Sales Price to Income
1954	$12,300	$ 4,173	2.95
1955	13,700	4,421	3.10
1956	14,300	4,783	2.99
1959	15,200	5,417	2.81
1963	18,000	6,249	2.88
1964	18,900	6,569	2.88
1965	20,000	6,957	2.87
1966	21,400	7,532	2.84
1967	22,700	7,933	2.86
1968	24,700	8,632	2.86
1969	25,600	9,433	2.71
1970	23,400	9,867	2.37
1971	25,200	10,285	2.45
1972	27,600	11,116	2.48
1973	32,500	12,051	2.70
1974	35,900	12,836	2.78
1975	39,300	13,719	2.86
1976	44,200	14,958	2.95
1977	48,800	16,009	3.05
1978	55,700	17,640	3.16
1979	62,900	19,661	3.20
1980	64,500	21,023	3.07

Source: U.S. Bureau of the Census, Department of Commerce. *Construction Reports,* "New One-Family Houses Sold and For Sale," Series C25 (Washington, D.C.: U.S. Government Printing Office, Monthly); U.S. Bureau of the Census, Department of Commerce. Current Population Reports Series P-60, *Money Income and Poverty Status of Families and Persons in the United States: Annual.* (Washington, D.C. Government Printing Office, Annual).

paying 35 percent or more of income for rent, totaling nearly 8 million by the end of the decade, almost one-third of all renters.

As is evident from Exhibit 62, it is only husband-and-wife households that, at least in the aggregate, have stayed below the 25 percent parameter. But this is the group that rapidly vacated rental housing over the decade. The most severely impacted, as would be implied from the analysis presented in chapter 7, are female-headed households, whose rents account for close to $4 out of every $10 of income. The deterioration of these relationships by household

EXHIBIT 60

Median Sales Price of New One-Family Houses Sold and Median Income, United States: 1975 and 1979

All Families

	Median Sales Price	Median Income	Ratio of Sales Price to Income
1975	$39,300	$13,719	2.86
1979	62,900	19,661	3.20

All Married-Couple Families

	Median Sales Price	Median Income	Ratio of Sales Price to Income
1975	$39,300	$14,867	2.64
1979	62,900	21,503	2.93

Married-Couple Families, Wife Employed Full Time

	Median Sales Price	Median Income	Ratio of Sales Price to Income
1975	$39,300	$18,262	2.15
1979	62,900	26,196	2.40

Married-Couple Families, Householder Year-Round Full-Time Worker, Wife Employed Full Time

	Median Sales Price	Median Income	Ratio of Sales Price to Income
1975	$39,300	$20,185	1.95
1979	62,900	28,189	2.23

Source: See Exhibits 43 and 45.

configuration over time are shown in Exhibit 63.

American households, regardless of their tenurial status, are finding it necessary to devote a greater portion of their income in order to secure shelter. It is the decline of housing buying power — whose full reality has been obscured to date by the benefits of increased levels of housing-price inflation to extant homeowners, but which now is evident — which sets the stage for housing starts and household configurations to come.

As we view the data, they call for increasing levels of market segmentation and certainly much more modest housing formats. While a great deal will depend on the future priorities granted to housing — particularly in terms of restructuring of financial markets — the assurance of housing affluence to come, based solely upon demographics, must be significantly questioned when it is tempered in the light of the overall economy.

EXHIBIT 61
Gross Rent as a Percent of Income:
Specified Renter Households — 1970 to 1979
(Numbers in Thousands)

	1970	1979	Change: 1970 to 1979 Number	Change: 1970 to 1979 Percent
Specified Renter Occupied	22,334	26,550	4,216	18.9%
less than 10 percent	2,012	1,249	-763	-37.9
10 to 14 percent	3,979	2,962	-1,017	-25.6
15 to 19 percent	3,786	4,109	323	8.5
20 to 24 percent	2,657	3,840	1,183	44.5
25 to 34 percent	2,936	4,974	2,038	69.4
35 percent or more	5,209	7,956	2,747	52.7
Not Computed	1,756	1,459	—	—
Median	20%	26%	6%	30.0%

Source: U.S. Department of Commerce, Bureau of the Census, *Current Housing Reports,* Series H-150-79, *Annual Housing Survey: 1979, Parts A and C.* U.S. Government Printing Office, Washington, D.C., 1981.

It is worthwhile in this context to review the household projections shown in Exhibit 20 of chapter 3. Those demographic sectors which have been the greatest consumers of homeownership (married couple families) should expand much more rapidly in the 1980s. But will this linkage continue? Moreover, questions can be raised as to the capacity of households to form at the rate experienced in earlier years, given the increased costs of housing-unit acquisition. Thus the very increments in housing costs, reflected in a downturn in new housing-unit production, may feed back on the household configurational growth which has been anticipated to drive the economic machine.

SUMMARY

The demographics of the 1970s were intimately linked to the corresponding housing parameters of the decade. But as the 1980s ensue, the latter have shifted markedly - the housing-buying power of Americans is declining. In turn, this will feed back and shape demographics to come, as well as future economic reality.

1. The 1970s in retrospect stand as America's golden housing era; a net increase of 20 million housing units was realized, virtually twice that of the 1960s.

EXHIBIT 62
Median Rent as a Percent of Income: U.S. Total, 1979

Household composition By Age of Head	1979 Median Income	1979 Median Monthly Gross Rent	1979 Median Annual Gross Rent	1979 Median Annual Rent as a Percent of Median Income
2-or-More Person Households	$11,600	$233	$2,796	24.1%
Male Head, Wife Present	14,200	237	2,844	20.0
Under 25 years	12,500	222	2,664	21.3
25 to 29 Years	15,200	241	2,892	19.0
30 to 34 Years	15,900	247	2,964	18.6
35 to 44 Years	16,400	260	3,120	19.0
45 to 64 Years	15,000	239	2,868	19.1
65 Years and Over	8,800	204	2,448	27.8
Other Male Head	10,800	255	3,060	28.3
Under 65 Years	11,000	258	3,096	28.1
65 Years and Over	6,900	178	2,136	31.0
Female Head	7,000	217	2,604	37.2
Under 65 Years	6,900	220	2,640	38.3
65 Years and Over	7,000	189	2,268	32.4
1-Person Households	7,500	189	2,268	30.2

Source: U.S. Department of Commerce, Bureau of the Census, *Current Housing Reports,* Series H-150-68, *Annual Housing Survey: 1979, Parts A and C.* U.S. Government Printing Office, Washington, D.C. 1981.

2. Five times during the decade, new, privately owned housing starts approached or exceeded an annual level of 2 million units. An inflation-driven housing-buying hysteria characterized the latter half of the 1970s, leading to record rates of homeownership.

3. Husband-wife households — the most affluent household format — rapidly withdrew from rental tenure. The latter increasingly became the province of the financially less well endowed — non-husband-wife household configurations. But such "non-modular" households also realized extensive ownership gains as well.
4. Soaring prices attached to home ownership served not as a retardant, but as an enhancer — an inflation-proof commodity desired by all Americans. But as the 1980s began, prices of single-family homes began to lag as new financing strictures emerged.

EXHIBIT 63
Renter Households, Median Rent as a Percent of Median Income: 1973, 1976 and 1979

Household Composition By Age of Head	1973	1976	1979
2-or-More Person Households	19.6%	22.6%	24.1%
Male Head, Wife Present	18.2	18.9	20.0
Under 25 Years	19.8	20.3	21.3
25 to 29 Years	17.4	18.3	19.0
30 to 34 Years	17.0	17.8	18.6
35 to 44 Years	17.1	17.7	19.0
45 to 64 Years	16.4	17.5	19.1
65 Years and Over	29.6	29.6	27.8
Other Male Head	21.0	26.3	28.3
Under 65 Years	20.7	26.2	28.1
65 Years and Over	28.0	28.8	31.0
Female Head	26.9	35.8	37.2
Under 65 Years	26.6	35.4	38.3
65 Years and Over	31.0	33.2	32.4
1-Person Households	30.7	31.0	30.2

Source: U.S. Department of Commerce, Bureau of the Census, *Current Housing Reports,* Series H-150-79, *Annual Housing Survey: 1979, Parts A and C.* U.S. Government Printing Office, Washington, D.C., 1981.

5. Long-term, fixed-rate mortgages at rates below inflation will be permanently relegated to history in the 1980s. Even new multiple year-round full-time worker households will find homeownership a financially hazardous undertaking, markedly altering consumption patterns.
6. The throughput of America's housing delivery system will not match the performance of the 1970s. There is a very real question as to whether it will even approach it during the 1980s. The feedback on demographics will be substantial, particularly in lowering the rate of household formation. Calibrating projection models on the baselines of the 1970s may lead to forecasts far at variance with reality to come.
7. Housing availability and demographic mobility are also linked phenomena. Certainly, the regional population movements documented in the following chapter were, at least in part, a consequence of the 1970s' housing boom. A restructured housing arena in the 1980s may retard spatial population movements.

Chapter Ten

CHANGING REGIONAL DISTRIBUTION: POPULATION

Spatial redistribution may accent or mute the immediacies of general population growth trends. Areas securing net inmigration can be faced with the prospect of educational-plant expansion while the nation as a whole experiences substantial contraction of its school-age population — or, for that matter, at the same time, areas of outmigration experience an immediate crisis of excess infrastructure.

Declining rates of net natural increase thrust migration into an increasingly prominent role in local growth determination. High rates of fertility tend to justify and confirm the vitality of established places, serving to mask the realities of declining areas or at least to obscure the necessities of acknowledging them. As birth rates wane, the decision of people to redistribute themselves — to migrate — becomes much more apparent and influential. The evolving geography of the nation's population refines and modifies the effects on individual political jurisdictions of the parameters and dynamics previously discussed, as well as spawning an array of additional concerns.

The spatial redistribution of America's citizenry, typified by suburban growth and central-city decline in the past three decades, is all too familiar, etched deeply into our day-to-day consciousness. While the history of the United States can be structured in terms of the complex ebbs and flows of migration, until recently, there has been a tendency to overlook the broader, more pervasive swings in population settlement. The classical analytical works on western expansion, for example, paralleled by the equivalent elaboration of the waves of European immigration that buffeted our cities, dominate the shelf with little on other areal partitions.

Their present-day equivalent — the regional dimension — has recently captured the fancy of the popular media, with "Sunbelt" and "Frostbelt" as new entries into the journalists' lexicon, serving as a current reference framework for domestic issues. The principal focus is on the territories being vacated — paralleled by fascination with the "new South" and energy-rich mountain states. This stands in contrast to the primary target of past historical consciousness, the waves and frontiers of growth. The one major exception has been the coverage given to the flight from the land — the great agricultural displacement of the 1930s and more recent periods. In any case, the regional shift, although linked to metropolitan and urban changes, promises to interpenetrate every dimension of national domestic policy, as well as influence the daily activities of planners and local political leadership, throughout the midterm future.

THE LONGER-TERM PATTERNS

As a backdrop to the new concerns of the 1980s, it is useful to examine the patterns of regional change for the two decades prior to 1970, the baseline of the present transformation. Exhibit 64 details the population changes which have taken place on a regional and divisional base between 1950 and 1970.[22] Between 1950 and 1960, the United States as a whole experienced a rate of growth of 18.5 percent and an absolute increase of 28 million people. The growth was relatively evenly shared (in total numbers) among the major regional clusters (between 7.2 million and 7.9 million) with the exception of the Northeast, which expanded by only 5.2 million people. Those areas trailing the national growth *rate* most severely were the industrialized Northeast (13.2 percent) and the agricultural states of the West North Central (9.5 percent) and East South Central (5.0 percent) Divisions. In contrast, the West was the fastest-growing area of the nation, increasing in size by 38.9 percent.

Between 1960 and 1970, regional disparities began to sharpen focus, with the Northeast and North Central regions differentiated from the South and West, lagging in both absolute growth and percentage change. Indeed, in the face of a shrinking national growth increment (24 million people), the South's net gain in population (7.9 million) was greater than that of the previous decade, the only region to experience an increasing level of absolute growth — and this despite the continued dissolution of labor-intensive farming in the East South Central division.

THE RECENT ACCELERATION

The trends evident in the two decades prior to 1970 foreshadowed the general pattern of events that were to take place in the 1970s, but not their scale and magnitude. A gradual and persistent evolution rapidly accelerated into a process of snowballing momentum. As Exhibit 65 indicates, the 1970 to 1980 growth rates of the South (20.0 percent) and West (23.9 percent) were

EXHIBIT 64

Regional Population Growth Patterns: 1950 to 1970
(Numbers in Thousands)

				Numerical Change		Percentage Change	
Region and Division	**1950[1]**	**1960[2]**	**1970[3]**	**1950-1960**	**1960-1970**	**1950-1960**	**1960-1970**
Northeast Region	39,478	44,678	49,061	5,200	4,383	13.2	9.8
New England	9,314	10,509	11,847	1,195	1,338	12.8	12.7
Middle Atlantic	30,164	34,168	37,213	4,004	3,045	13.3	8.9
North Central Region	44,461	51,619	56,590	7,158	4,971	16.1	9.6
East North Central	30,399	36,225	40,263	5,826	4,038	19.2	11.2
West North Central	14,061	15,394	16,328	1,333	934	9.5	6.1
South Region	46,197	54,961	62,813	7,764	7,852	16.5	14.3
South Atlantic	21,182	25,959	30,679	4,777	4,720	22.6	18.2
East South Central	11,477	12,050	12,808	573	758	5.0	6.3
West South Central	14,538	16,951	19,326	2,413	2,375	16.6	14.0
West Region	20,190	28,053	34,838	7,863	6,785	38.9	24.2
Mountain	5,075	6,855	8,290	1,780	1,435	35.1	20.9
Pacific	15,115	21,198	26,548	6,083	5,350	40.2	25.2
U.S. TOTAL	151,326	179,311	203,302	27,985	23,991	18.5	13.4

Notes: [1]April 1, 1950 Census.
[2]April 1, 1960 Census, as reported by source below.
[3]April 1, 1970 Census, as reported by source below.

Source: U.S. Bureau of the Census, Current Population Reports, Series P-20, No. 363, *Population Profile of the United States: 1980,* U.S. Government Printing Office, Washington, D.C., 1981.

more than a hundred times greater than that of the Northeast (0.2 percent) and over five times greater than the North Central region (4.0 percent). Lagging most severely were the highly industrialized states of the Middle Atlantic and East North Central divisions, the historic manufacturing belt of America stretching from New York to Chicago.

The improved relative performance of the West South Central and East South Central divisions gives some indication that the phenomenon of rural agricultural displacement has ended; the latter is no longer available to bolster the sagging populations of the Northern industrial cities. Secondly, the former territories, having "unloaded" their "redundant" populations, had set the stage for improved growth performance.

The energy and natural-resources crises of the 1970s improved the economic status of those states which serve as exporters of these vital commodities. Not only is this phenomenon reflected in the Southern divisions cited above, but also in the Mountain states — whose growth rate (37.1 percent)

EXHIBIT 65

Regional Population Growth Patterns: 1970 to 1980

(Numbers in Thousands)

			Change 1970-1980		Change 1960-1970
Region and Division	**1970[1]**	**1980[2]**	**Number**	**Percent**	**Percent**
U.S. TOTAL	203,302	226,505	23,203	11.4	13.4
Northeast Region	49,061	49,137	76	0.2	9.8
New England	11,847	12,348	501	4.2	12.7
Middle Atlantic	37,213	36,788	-425	-1.1	8.9
North Central Region	56,590	58,854	2,264	4.0	9.6
East North Central	40,263	41,670	1,407	3.5	11.1
West North Central	16,328	17,184	857	5.2	6.1
South Region	62,813	75,349	12,536	20.0	14.3
South Atlantic	30,679	36,943	6,264	20.4	18.2
East South Central	12,808	14,663	1,855	14.5	6.3
West South Central	19,326	23,743	4,417	22.9	14.0
West Region	34,838	43,165	8,327	23.9	24.2
Mountain	8,290	11,368	3,078	37.1	20.9
Pacific	26,548	31,797	5,249	19.8	25.2

Note: [1]April 1, 1970 Census as reported by source below.
[2]April 1, 1980 Census as reported by source below.

Source: U.S. Bureau of the Census, Current Population Reports, Series P-20, No. 363, *Population Profile of the United States: 1980,* U.S. Government Printing Office, Washington, D.C., 1981.

was the highest in the nation. For the first time it eclipsed that of the Pacific division (19.8 percent) — and the oil- and natural-gas-rich territories of the West South Central division.

Thus, the rise of the Sunbelt and the stagnation of the Northeast and North Central states represent deepening contours on America's population landscape. Exhibit 66 provides an alternate perspective on this development, indicating the shares of national growth secured by each region and division for the three periods under consideration (1950 to 1960, 1960 to 1970, and 1970 to 1980). Again, the data emphasize one of the hazards of forecasting: that of being right in direction but wrong in time, scale, and dimension. While the earlier data made apparent the shifts in regional growth (at least in hindsight), the future (1980) actually arrived much faster than any but the most omniscient seer could have anticipated. The bulk of the national population growth from 1970 to 1980 was the province of the South (54.0 percent) and West (36.9 percent).

The central city-suburban bifurcation of the past three decades has now been amplified to the national scale with the older Northern sectors of the country in the central-city role. The flows of population have been so dramatic

EXHIBIT 66

Region and Division Percentage Shares of National Growth 1950 to 1980

	Period		
Region and Division	**1950 - 1960**	**1960 - 1970**	**1970 - 1980**
Northeast Region	18.6	18.3	0.3
New England	4.3	5.6	2.2
Middle Atlantic	14.3	12.7	-1.8
North Central Region	25.6	20.7	9.8
East North Central	20.8	16.8	6.1
West South Central	4.8	3.9	3.7
South Region	27.7	32.7	54.0
South Atlantic	17.1	19.7	27.0
East South Central	2.0	3.2	8.0
West South Central	8.6	9.9	19.0
West Region	28.1	28.3	36.9
Mountain	6.4	6.0	13.3
Pacific	21.7	22.3	22.6
U.S. TOTAL	100.0	100.0	100.0

Source: Derived from Exhibits 64 and 65.

as to make obsolete many of the concepts of market analysts. The potency of the flywheels set in motion is illustrated by their internal dynamics.

THE COMPONENTS OF CHANGE

The declining fertility rates documented previously affect the balance of the two components of population growth — net natural increase and net migration — as they are manifested in each regional territory. Exhibit 67 presents the absolute population change for each region for each five-year-period between July 1, 1950, and April 1, 1980. (It should be emphasized that for the three previous exhibits the April 1 benchmark was used for 1970 and prior years.) These increments, while replicating information previously reviewed, provide the base for disaggregation into the components of change, the subject of Exhibit 68.

After reaching its maximum in the 1955-to-1960 period — when the birth rate peaked — population growth due to net natural increase declined in each succeeding five-year period in every region, both in terms of absolute size and as a percentage of the population base at the beginning year of each period (Exhibit 68). At the same time, there has been a tendency for net migration to increase over the past decade. Particularly significant is the net inmigration of 4.1 million people to the South between 1970 and 1979; the latter has reached parity with the historic magnet (the West) in capturing the bulk of the nation's movers. Indeed, in the space of one generation, the South has evolved from a situation of heavy outmigration losses to very substantial inmigration gains.

In the years between 1955 and 1970, the South maintained a slight positive net migration despite the trek north of its rural black population — the terminal shift of population as a function of the agricultural revolution. Only the large influx of people moving to Florida over this period dampened the overall migration implications of the latter phenomenon.[23]

Particularly striking in this context is the selective migration of the elderly shown in Exhibit 69. The South clearly was the leading beneficiary of differential interregional shifts while the Northeast and North Central regions were the major losers. In the former case, from 1975 to 1979, 132,000 elderly individuals (65 years of age and over) migrated from the Northeast to the South with an additional 95,000 arriving from the North Central region. The skew in origin is reversed when the pattern of inmigration to the West is considered. In this case, 13,000 Northeasterners moved to the West while the flow from the North Central region was almost seven times that, or 80,000.

Conversely, inmigration to the Northeast from other regions was relatively trivial (39,000), while the North Central states secured but 67,000 elderly inmigrants. Thus, the patterns of preference are most clear. With early retirement clearly expanding, this type of preferential relocation may take on added significance in the years to come.

Migration is a telling criterion of location shift by choice, of people seeking

EXHIBIT 67

Population Change for Five-Year Periods by Region: 1950 to 1980

(Periods Beginning July 1. Change Expressed in Millions)

Period	U.S. Total	Northeast Region	North Central Region	South Region	West Region
1950-1955	13.2	2.7	3.9	2.9	3.7
1955-1960	14.9	2.5	3.2	5.0	4.2
1960-1965	13.5	2.6	2.5	4.4	3.9
1965-1970	10.4	1.7	2.4	3.4	2.8
1970-1975[1]	12.2	0.4	1.3	6.8	3.7
1975-1980[1]	11.0	-0.3	1.0	5.8	4.6

Note: [1]Based on April 1 for 1970 and 1980, and on July 1 for 1975.

Source: U.S. Bureau of the Census, Current Population Reports, Series P-25, No. 640, *Estimates of the Population of States with Components of Change: 1970 to 1975,* U.S. Government Printing Office, Washington, D.C., 1976; and, press release of Census Bureau.

EXHIBIT 68

Population Change by Component by Region: 1950 to 1979[1,2]

(Numbers in Millions)

	Net Natural Increase					Net Migration				
		Region					Region			
Period	United States	Northeast	North Central	South	West	United States	Northeast	North Central	South	West
1950-1955	12.1	2.3	3.5	4.5	1.9	1.0	0.4	0.4	-1.6	1.9
1955-1960	13.2	2.6	3.9	4.7	2.2	1.7	(Z)[3]	-0.7	0.3	2.0
1960-1965	12.0	2.3	3.3	4.2	2.2	1.5	0.3	-0.8	0.3	1.7
1965-1970	8.7	1.6	2.3	3.0	1.7	1.7	0.1	0.1	0.4	1.1
1970-1975	7.3	1.1	2.0	2.7	1.6	2.4	-0.8	-0.9	2.6	1.5
1975-1979	5.5	0.7	1.4	1.9	1.4	1.6	-1.0	-0.7	1.5	1.8
	Percent of Population Base at Beginning Year of Period									
1950-1955	8.0%	5.9%	7.7%	9.5%	9.1%	0.7%	1.0%	0.9%	-3.5%	9.2%
1955-1960	8.0	6.1	7.9	9.2	9.1	1.0	-0.1	-1.3	0.6	8.5
1960-1965	6.7	5.2	6.4	7.5	7.7	0.8	0.7	-1.6	0.5	6.2
1965-1970	4.5	3.4	4.3	5.1	5.3	0.9	0.2	0.2	0.7	3.3
1970-1975	3.6	2.2	3.5	4.3	4.6	1.2	-1.7	-1.6	4.1	4.4
1975-1979	2.6	1.4	2.4	2.8	3.7	0.7	-2.0	-1.2	2.2	4.7

Notes: [1]Data for the periods 1950 through 1970 are as of July 1; data for the periods 1970 through 1979 are as of April 1 for 1970 and July 1 for 1975 and 1979.

[2]Data in this exhibit are not strictly comparable to data in previous exhibits.

[3]Z indicates less than 50,000.

Source: U.S. Bureau of the Census, Current Population Reports, Series P-25, No. 640, *Estimates of the Population of States with Components of Change: 1970 to 1975,* U.S. Government Printing Office, Washington, D.C., 1976; and U.S. Bureau of the Census, Current Population Reports, Series P-25, No. 876, *Annual Estimates of the Population of States: July 1, 1970 to 1979 with Components of Change, 1970 to 1979,* U.S. Government Printing Office, Washington, D.C., 1980.

EXHIBIT 69
Region of Residence in March 1975 and March 1979 for Migrants 65 Years of Age and Over[1]
(Numbers in Thousands)[2,3]

Region of Residence in 1979	Total Migrants	Region of Residence in 1975: Northeast	North Central	South	West
United States	1,707	381	461	535	331
Northeast	268	229	6	28	5
North Central	347	7	280	52	8
South	670	132	95	416	27
West	423	13	80	39	291
Percent Distribution					
United States	100.0%	22.3%	27.0%	31.3%	19.4%
Northeast	100.0	85.4	2.2	10.4	1.9
North Central	100.0	2.0	80.7	15.0	2.3
South	100.0	19.7	14.2	62.1	4.0
West	100.0	3.1	18.9	9.1	68.8

Notes: [1]Migrants are all persons who, at the end of the period, were living in a county in the United States different from that they lived in at the beginning of the period.
[2]Numbers and percents may not sum because of rounding.
[3]Data in this exhibit may not be strictly comparable to data in previous exhibits.

Source: U.S. Bureau of the Census, Current Population Reports, Series P-20, No. 353, *Geographic Mobility: March 1975 to March 1979,* U.S. Government Printing Office, Washington, D.C., 1980.

out "better" places to live. The current preferences of Americans are clearly gauged by the data of Exhibits 68 and 69, with the aging industrial belt being vacated as a matter of conscious choice.

SUMMARY

The secular pattern of population shift in the United States — as exemplified by the advancing western frontier — has been suddenly accentuated. The declining rates and magnitudes of net natural increase have increased the import of migration as a source of population growth. And as a matter of affirmative individual decision making, the Sunbelt has gained supremacy as a residential environment of choice.

1. The long-term trend (1950 to 1980) shows the Northeast and North Central

states with decreasing shares of declining national growth, while the South and West have increasingly secured the bulk of America's population growth, from 55.8 percent in the 1950 to 1960 period, to 61.0 percent over the following decade, and to 89.9 percent in the 1970 to 1980 period.

2. The latter acceleration promises to be one of the hallmarks of the 1980s. From 1975 to 1979, the South and West experienced a net inmigration of 3.3 million individuals while the Northeast and North Central regions were buffeted by losses of 1.7 million outmigrants. And the latter indicator may actually underestimate the problems of the aging industrial states, since the United States as a whole experienced a 1.6-million-person increase in population due to overseas migration patterns.[24]
3. Nevertheless, the impetus to flee settings thought of as undesirable socially and environmentally for more attractive alternatives has been expanded to greater spatial scales. Suburban flight has given way to regional shift.
4. Population shifts serve as both signal and instigator of both economic growth and decline. Certainly, patterns of economic growth and spatial redistribution are highly correlated to the population complement (chapter 11). But in the context of population-serving economic activity — retailing, for example —population flows foster the rapid replication of facilities left behind, often underutilized or vacated as their economic rationale is removed. The fractured landscapes of many declining Northern cities bear testimony to the residual effects of population shifts.
5. And in the context of the evolving age structure of America's population, which is generating excess capacity in many public facilities and infrastructures — schools, for example — at the aggregate national scale, the sheer magnitude of these population movements implies the necessityof public expenditure in growth territories to replicate the same operations and facilities already existing in vacated territories. Yet the latter are not easily scaled down nor abrogated without adding impetus to the very process of decline.

Chapter Eleven

CHANGING REGIONAL DISTRIBUTION: EMPLOYMENT

The increasing dominance by the South and West of national population growth as well as housing starts — and the recent regional shifts in single-family-unit sales prices — is closely paralleled by the changing regional distribution of job growth. While much of the economic trauma of the older regions surfaced during the national recession of 1974-1975, the basic phenomenon, in less severe form, persisted before and after this "crisis."

But it was during the recession that the long-term transformation in the nation's social and economic parameters came under scrutiny. The aging industrial heartland of America — stretching from New England to the upper Midwest — began to experience unique strains emanating from economic contraction and population migration to the national Sunbelt. The traditional bases of industrial America have become prisoners of their early history and are experiencing the dislocations caused by accelerating technological change, a maturing economy and, subject to recession-induced caution, a mobile and footloose population.

This chapter will analyze regional employment shifts over the 1960 to 1981 period according to the employment partitions utilized in chapter 6 — manufacturing, private nonmanufacturing, and government. Before these individual sectors are examined, however, the pattern of total employment change by region and division is reviewed.

TOTAL EMPLOYMENT CHANGE BY REGION AND DIVISION

In Exhibit 70 is shown total employment change from 1960 to 1975 and from 1975 to 1981 for the major regions and divisions of the United States. The first fifteen years from 1960 to 1975 encompass a period in which the total

EXHIBIT 70

Total Employment Change: 1960-1981[1] By Region and Division

(Numbers in Thousands)

Region and Division	1960	1975	Change 1960-1975 Number	Change 1960-1975 Percent	1981	Change 1975-1981 Number	Change 1975-1981 Percent
Northeast Region	15,229.5	18,535.4	3,305.9	21.7	20,354.8	1,819.4	9.8
Middle Atlantic Division	11,676.4	13,864.9	2,188.5	18.7	14,884.1	1,019.2	7.4
New England Division	3,553.1	4,670.5	1,117.4	31.4	5,470.7	800.2	17.1
North Central Region	15,291.8	20,826.7	5,534.9	36.2	23,375.2	2,548.5	12.2
East North Central Division	11,318.1	14,957.5	3,639.4	32.2	16,578.7	1,621.2	10.8
West North Central Division	3,973.7	5,869.2	1,895.5	47.7	6,776.5	927.3	15.8
South Region	13,818.0	23,480.3	9,662.3	69.9	29,453.8	5,973.5	25.4
South Atlantic Division	7,054.2	12,078.8	5,024.6	71.2	14,790.8	2,712.0	22.5
East South Central Division	2,606.0	4,353.0	1,747.0	67.0	5,086.9	733.9	16.9
West South Central Division	4,157.8	7,048.5	2,890.7	69.5	9,576.1	2,527.6	35.9
West Region	7,734.3	13,110.4	5,376.1	69.5	17,025.2	3,914.8	29.9
Mountain Division	1,765.9	3,353.9	1,588.0	89.9	4,509.0	1,155.1	34.4
Pacific Division	5,968.4	9,756.5	3,788.1	63.5	12,516.2	2,759.7	28.3
U.S. Total[2]	52,073.6	75,952.8	23,879.2	46.6	90,209.0	14,256.2	18.8

Notes: [1]Employees on nonagriculture payrolls as of March of the respective years.
[2]Excludes Hawaii and Alaska.

Source: U.S. Department of Labor, Bureau of Labor Statistics, *Employment and Earnings* (Washington, D.C.: U.S. Government Printing Office, Monthly).

employment base of the United States increased by 46.6 percent. There was, however, significant regional variation. The Northeast, for example, secured less than half (21.7 percent) the percentage increment enjoyed by the nation as a whole, with the Middle Atlantic division (New Jersey, New York, and Pennsylvania) the slowest-growing sector of the country, showing a growth rate of less than one in five — 18.7 percent. The North Central region, while faring somewhat better (36.2 percent), also lagged behind the national pace of growth. The rise of the Sunbelt was marked by the South's securing nearly 10 million additional jobs (69.9 percent), with the West nearly matching the percentage increment (69.5 percent), although its absolute growth, 5.4 million new jobs, is smaller. The "Frostbelt" — or Northeast region — by way of contrast, gained barely a third the number of jobs secured in the South and only 60 percent that of the West.

The situation from 1975 to 1981 very largely continued the trends established in the earlier period. The nation as a whole in that six-year period had an employment increase of 18.8 percent — or slightly more than 14 million new jobs. But the Northeast again grew at half the national rate (9.8 percent) while its Middle Atlantic Division again grew at an even slower pace (7.4 percent). The North Central region continued to follow the pattern of the Northeast (12.2 percent) as the South (25.4 percent) and West (29.9 percent) continued to dominate the nation.

In 1960, the Northeast with over 15 million jobs closely matched the North Central region as the top employment node of the country. The South lagged well behind (13.8 million) while the West had less than half of the Northeast total (7.7 million). By 1981, the balance sheet had been remarkably altered. The Northeast had fallen well behind the North Central region and had barely two-thirds of the jobs held in the South, while the West was moving much closer to parity. Thus the general vision of a burgeoning Sunbelt and a lagging Northeast is borne out in the national statistical employment accounts.

Inter-Period Variations

These trends are further clarified in the data of Exhibit 71 which indicate regional growth shares of total employment change for the five-year periods from 1960 through 1975 as well as for the six-year interval from 1975 to 1981. Clearly, each of the periods under scrutiny reflects very different growth characteristics, with the national economic cycles basically defining the individual regional variations, but the latter in turn possessing underlying growth dynamics of their own.

The weakness of the Northeast and the growing strength of the South was clear from 1960 to 1965, a period of only modest national performance. The former accounted for only 14.5 percent of the nation's employment gains, while the latter garnered 38.5 percent. The boom period of 1965 to 1970

EXHIBIT 71

Regional Growth Shares of Total Employment Change: 1960-1981[1]

(Numbers in Thousands)

	Absolute Growth Increment				Percentage Share of National Growth			
Region and Division	**1960-1965**	**1965-1970**	**1970-1975**	**1975-1981**	**1960-1965**	**1965-1970**	**1970-1975**	**1975-1981**
Northeast Region	875.7	2,465.9	-35.7	1,819.4	14.5	20.7	-0.6	12.8
Middle Atlantic Division	594.2	1,818.2	-223.9	1,019.2	9.8	15.3	-3.8	7.1
New England Division	281.5	647.7	188.2	800.2	4.7	5.4	3.2	5.6
North Central Region	1,422.2	3,240.6	872.1	2,548.5	23.6	27.2	14.7	17.9
East Central Division	989.7	2,332.6	317.6	1,621.2	16.4	19.6	5.4	11.4
West North Central Division	432.5	980.5	554.5	927.3	7.2	7.6	9.4	6.5
South Region	2,323.6	4,033.6	3,305.1	5,973.5	38.5	33.9	55.8	41.9
South Atlantic Division	1,182.8	2,146.6	1,695.2	2,712.0	19.6	18.0	28.6	19.0
East South Central Division	509.4	668.5	569.1	733.9	8.4	5.6	9.6	5.1
West South Central Division	631.4	1,218.5	1,040.8	2,527.6	10.5	10.2	17.6	17.7
West Region	1,420.4	2,171.3	1,784.4	3,914.8	23.5	18.2	30.1	27.5
Mountain Division	322.8	493.7	771.5	1,155.1	5.3	4.1	13.0	8.1
Pacific Division	1,097.6	1,677.6	1,012.9	2,759.7	18.2	14.1	17.1	19.4
U.S. Total[2]	6,041.9[3]	11,911.4	5,925.9	14,256.2	100.0	100.0	100.0	100.0

Notes: [1]Employees on nonagriculture payrolls as of March of the respective periods.
[2]Excludes Hawaii and Alaska.
[3]Numbers and percents may not add due to rounding.

Source: U.S. Department of Labor, Bureau of Labor Statistics, *Employment and Earnings* (Washington, D.C.: U.S. Government Printing Office, Monthly).

obscured this differential, dampening the interregional spread. Yet the South still secured 33.9 percent of the nation's growth.

Much of the difficulty of the Northeast and the Middle Atlantic states has been attributed to the sluggish national performance of the 1970 to 1975 period, when the total employment gains of the nation (5.9 million jobs) dropped to half the level (11.9 million) of the preceding five years (1965 to 1970). Indeed, the Northeast region had gained 2.5 million jobs in the first period, only to lose 35,700 over the 1970 to 1975 period. Thus when the nation's economy stagnated, the older regions' (Northeast and North Central) growth shares plummeted, while those of the South and West surged.

The reverse phenomenon occurred in the national job boom (14.3 million) of 1975 to 1981. But the shares of the Northeast and North Central states failed to return to the levels secured in the preceding high-growth era (1965 to 1970). Thus national strength lessened the trauma of the older regions, but did not fully meliorate it.

As we view the 21-year-period as a whole, the great costs of the 1974-1975 recession — most specifically to the Northeast region and Middle Atlantic division — become evident. Whether the 1980s will repeat the pattern of the last decade at the low points of the economc cycle remains a question of compelling urgency.

MANUFACTURING EMPLOYMENT

Despite the rise of the post-industrial or service economy, it is manufacturing which is still a basic underlying element, both directly and indirectly, as a multiplier for other activities as well as providing general insight into the shifting patterns of industrialization and service employment for the nation and its constituents.

Exhibit 72 provides data on manufacturing employment change by region and division for the same time periods as earlier discussed. When the national totals in this sector are examined, it is evident that we have long since moved from a national economy dominated by manufacturing employment. Total employment in this sector grew by less than 10 percent from 1960 to 1975 — and only slightly more than that threshold in the six years from 1975 to 1981.

The earlier period (1960 to 1975) was marked by very abrupt manufacturing declines within the Northeast region, with a loss of nearly one in six jobs (-13.9 percent) or an average of 1 percent a year. Between 1975 and 1981, however, with a much more vigorous general economy, a near bottoming out of the decline in the region was approached. But during both of these periods, the South and West secured the bulk of new manufacturing activity.

It is important in this context to stress the significant turnaround that has been demonstrated by the New England division's manufacturing sector. From 1960 to 1975, this area lost more than one in ten (-10.8 percent) of its manufacturing jobs. This trend was reversed from 1975 to 1981 by an increase

EXHIBIT 72

Manufacturing Employment Change: 1960-1981[1] by Region
(Numbers in Thousands)

Region and Division	1960	1975	Change 1960-1975 Number	Change 1960-1975 Percent	1981	Change 1975-1981 Number	Change 1975-1981 Percent
Northeast Region	5,620.6	4,839.2	-781.4	-13.9	5,016.2	177.0	3.7
Middle Atlantic Division	4,172.8	3,547.1	-625.7	-15.0	3,503.9	-43.2	-1.2
New England Division	1,447.8	1,292.1	-155.7	-10.8	1,512.3	220.2	17.0
North Central Region	5,579.9	5,814.3	234.4	4.2	5,991.8	177.5	3.1
East North Central Division	4,586.4	4,577.8	8.6	-0.2	4,644.6	66.8	1.5
West North Central Division	993.5	1,236.5	243.0	24.5	1,347.2	110.7	8.9
South Region	3,650.5	5,146.5	1,496.0	41.0	6,082.4	935.9	18.2
South Atlantic Division	2,013.1	2,614.2	601.1	29.9	3,040.4	426.2	16.3
East South Central Division	823.2	1,245.0	421.8	51.2	1,350.9	105.9	8.5
West South Central Division	814.2	1,287.3	473.1	58.1	1,691.1	403.8	31.4
West Region	1,874.6	2,394.9	520.3	27.8	3,043.0	648.1	27.1
Mountain Division	248.9	411.2	162.3	65.2	564.9	153.7	37.4
Pacific Division	1,625.7	1,983.7	358.0	22.0	2,478.1	494.4	24.9
U.S. Total[2]	16,725.6	18,194.9	1,469.3	8.8	20,133.4	1,938.5	10.7

Notes: [1]Employees on nonagriculture payrolls as of March of the respective years.
[2]Excludes Hawaii and Alaska.

Source: U.S. Department of Labor, Bureau of Labor Statistics, *Employment and Earnings* (Washington, D.C.: U.S. Government Printing Office, Monthly).

of more than one in six jobs (17.0 percent), reflecting the emergence of new growth elements — particularly in electronics and computer manufacture — much of which was gestated in the research and development areas of Route 128 — the Boston metropolitan circumferential freeway. This seemingly moribund area secured an increase in manufacturing employment (17.0 percent) well over one and one half times the equivalent for the nation as a whole (10.7 percent), and indeed compared quite closely to the South region (18.2 percent), recently envisioned as the premier growth arena for blue-collar employment.

Intra-Period Variations

Thus, as shown in Exhibit 73, the New England division accounted for more than 11 percent of the total national growth in manufacturing employment from 1975 to 1981 after having been a substantial net loser in the 15 years preceding that period. The Middle Atlantic division, conversely, tied to older forms of manufacturing, began to resemble the New England of several generations ago, when it was losing textiles and other labor-intensive industries to the South and other regions.

But much of this stability in the older regions (Northeast and North Central) in the 1975 to 1981 period may solely be a consequence of an improved national posture. Indeed, the four periods presented in Exhibit 73 show that manufacturing employment in the Northeast and North Central regions fluctuated between slow growth and actual decline in concert with national growth cycles. In contrast, the pattern of the South and West fluctuated between slow and fast growth. The regional manufacturing divergence persisted through all four periods.

PRIVATE NONMANUFACTURING EMPLOYMENT CHANGE

It is nonmanufacturing activity that increasingly represents the bulk of the new employment opportunities for Americans (see chapter 6). In 1960, the manufacturing sector accounted for slightly more than 16.7 million jobs. Private nonmanufacturing at the same time had broached the 27 million mark. By 1981, the gap had broadened substantially. The former had increased only to 20 million jobs while the latter more than doubled to 53 million (Exhibit 74). Thus the United States, as an advanced, highly developed technological society, has rapidly moved from one in which employment is dominated by manufacturing to a post-industrial era of services and allied activities (see chapter 6).

But the same regional divergence documented previously is also manifest in the private nonmanufacturing sector. For both periods shown in Exhibit 74, the Northeast and North Central regions demonstrate rates of increase con-

EXHIBIT 73

Regional Growth Shares of Manufacturing Employment Change: 1960-1981[1]

(Numbers in Thousands)

	Absolute Growth Increment				Percentage Share of National Growth			
Region and Division	**1960-1965**	**1965-1970**	**1970-1975**	**1975-1981**	**1960-1965**	**1965-1970**	**1970-1975**	**1975-1981**
Northeast Region	-110.1	264.9	-936.2	177.0	-15.2	12.0	-63.8	9.1
Middle Atlantic Division	-89.4	187.8	-724.1	-43.2	-12.4	8.5	-49.4	-2.2
New England Division	-20.7	77.1	-212.1	220.2	-2.8	3.5	-14.4	11.4
North Central Region	189.7	624.5	-579.8	177.5	26.2	28.2	-39.5	9.2
East Central Division	148.0	428.0	-585.4	66.8	20.5	19.3	39.9	3.4
West North Central Division	41.7	195.7	5.6	110.7	5.8	8.8	0.4	5.7
South Region	520.6	951.6	23.9	935.9	72.0	43.0	1.6	48.3
South Atlantic Division	250.4	424.3	-73.6	426.2	34.6	19.2	-5.0	21.9
East South Central Division	157.1	233.3	31.4	105.9	21.7	10.5	2.1	5.5
West South Central Division	113.1	293.9	66.1	403.8	15.6	13.3	4.5	20.8
West Region	122.7	372.5	25.1	648.1	17.0	16.8	1.7	33.4
Mountain Division	25.4	82.9	54.0	153.7	3.5	3.7	3.7	7.9
Pacific Division	97.3	289.6	-28.9	494.7	13.5	13.1	-2.0	25.5
U.S. Total[2]	722.9[3]	2,213.4	-1,467.0	1,938.5	100.0	100.0	-100.0	100.0

Notes: [1]Employees on nonagriculture payrolls as of March of the respective periods.
[2]Excludes Hawaii and Alaska.
[3]Numbers and percents may not add due to rounding.

Source: U.S. Department of Labor, Bureau of Labor Statistics, *Employment and Earnings* (Washington, D.C.: U.S. Government Printing Office, Monthly).

EXHIBIT 74

Private Non-Manufacturing Employment Change: 1960-1981
by Region and Division
(Numbers in Thousands)

			Change 1960-1975			Change 1975-1981	
Region and Division	**1960**	**1975**	**Number**	**Percent**	**1981**	**Number**	**Percent**
Northeast Region	7,672.4	10,470.5	2,798.1	36.5	11,917.7	1,447.2	13.8
Middle Atlantic Division	6,025.2	7,847.0	1,821.8	30.2	8,795.1	948.1	12.1
New England Division	1,647.2	2,623.5	976.3	59.3	3,122.6	499.1	19.0
North Central Region	7,512.5	11,311.6	3,799.1	50.6	13,310.8	1,999.2	17.7
East North Central Division	5,252.6	7,876.2	2,623.6	49.9	9,165.8	1,289.6	16.4
West North Central Division	2,259.6	3,435.4	1,175.5	52.0	4,145.0	709.6	20.7
South Region	7,547.4	13,415.7	5,868.3	77.8	17,430.8	4,015.1	29.9
South Atlantic Division	3,694.0	6,802.4	3,108.4	84.1	8,622.1	1,819.7	26.8
East South Central Division	1,285.5	2,243.4	957.9	74.5	2,678.6	435.2	19.4
West South Central Division	2,567.9	4,369.9	1,802.0	70.2	6,130.1	1,760.2	40.3
West Region	4,326.3	7,792.8	3,466.5	80.1	10,684.8	2,892.0	37.1
Mountain Division	1,113.9	2,136.5	1,022.6	91.8	2,987.8	851.3	39.8
Pacific Division	3,212.4	5,656.9	2,443.9	76.1	7,697.0	2,040.7	36.1
U.S. Total[2]	27,058.6	42,990.6	15,932.9	58.9	53,344.1	10,353.5	24.1

Notes: [1]Employees on nonagriculture payrolls as of March of the respective years.
[2]Excludes Hawaii and Alaska.

Source: U.S. Department of Labor, Bureau of Labor Statistics, *Employment and Earnings* (Washington, D.C.: U.S. Government Printing Office, Monthly).

siderably below that of the nation; the converse is true for the South and West. This reflects not only the economic attractiveness of the Sunbelt territories, but also the stimulus of rapid and substantial population growth, which spawns the population-service employment encompassed in the nonmanufacturing classification.

Intra-Period Variations

While absolute declines are not registered in the four time periods detailed in Exhibit 75, the private nonmanufacturing sector was still subject to variations of national economic tides. Again, these were much more apparent in the growth increments of the older regions. In both the South and West, each succeeding time period between 1960-1965 and 1975-1981 showed larger absolute increments than their predecessors. In any case, the employment growth in this sector has served barely to counterbalance manufacturing stagnation in the Northeast and North Central regions, while enhancing the growth dynamic in the South and West.

TOTAL GOVERNMENT EMPLOYMENT

The period from 1960 to 1975 was an era characterized by marked increases in government employment (Exhibit 76). Accelerated by the necessities of coping with the baby boom, as well as the rise of a variety of publicly financed social programs, total national employment in this sector increased by more than 6.4 million jobs or 78.0 percent. While there was some evidence of a slowdown over the following six years (1975 to 1981), the net national gain was still close to 2 million jobs (13.3 percent).

However, interregional variations widened in the late 1970s. In the 1960 to 1975 period, the growth rates of the Northeast (66.6 percent) and North Central (68.3 percent) Regions were more competitive with the South (87.7 percent) and West (90.6 percent) than was the case of the preceding job sectors. However, from 1975 to 1981, the growth rates of the South (20.8 percent), for example, was more than triple that of the Northeast (6.1 percent).

Intra-period Variations

It is the new growth territories of the United States in which govenment employment is increasing most rapidly (Exhibit 77). In the 1960 to 1965 period, the South captured 32.9 percent of government-employment growth; this share surged to 52.1 percent during the 1975 to 1981 period. In contrast, the Northeast's share for the corresponding time periods declined from 20.5 percent to 9.9 percent. It should be noted in this context that, while there has been substantial criticism of the allocation of federal government jobs by region, much of the above pattern is a function both of employment growth

EXHIBIT 75

Regional Growth Shares of Private Non Manufacturing Employment Change: 1960-1981[1]
(Numbers in Thousands)

	Absolute Growth Increment				Percentage Share of National Growth			
Region and Division	**1960-1965**	**1965-1970**	**1970-1975**	**1975-1981**	**1960-1965**	**1965-1970**	**1970-1975**	**1975-1981**
Northeast Region	661.7	1,628.7	507.7	1,447.2	17.6	23.9	9.4	13.9
Middle Atlantic Division	425.8	1,174.0	222.0	948.1	11.3	17.2	4.1	9.2
New England Division	235.9	454.7	285.7	499.1	6.2	6.6	5.3	4.8
North Central Region	585.6	1,813.9	1,126.6	1,999.2	22.9	26.6	20.9	19.3
East Central Division	589.0	1,327.5	706.9	1,289.6	15.7	19.5	13.1	12.5
West North Central Division	269.0	486.8	419.6	709.6	7.1	7.1	7.8	6.9
South Region	1,283.1	2,151.6	2,433.6	4,015.1	34.2	31.6	45.2	38.8
South Atlantic Division	655.7	1,188.3	1,264.4	1,819.7	17.4	17.4	23.5	17.6
East South Central Division	249.1	297.5	411.3	435.2	6.6	4.3	7.6	4.2
West South Central Division	378.3	655.8	757.9	1,760.2	10.0	9.7	14.0	17.0
West Region	945.4	1,209.8	1,311.3	2,892.0	25.2	17.7	24.3	27.9
Mountain Division	209.8	253.9	558.9	851.3	5.5	3.7	10.3	8.2
Pacific Division	735.6	955.9	752.4	2,040.7	19.1	14.0	13.9	19.7
U.S. Total[2]	3,748.8	6,804.0	5,379.2	10,353.5	100.0	100.0	100.0	100.0

Notes: [1]Employees on nonagriculture payrolls as of March of the respective periods.
[2]Excludes Hawaii and Alaska.

Source: U.S. Department of Labor, Bureau of Labor Statistics, *Employment and Earnings* (Washington, D.C.: U.S. Government Printing Office, Monthly).

EXHIBIT 76

Total Government Employment Change: 1960-1981[1]
by Region and Division
(Numbers in Thousands)

Region and Division	1960	1975	Change 1960-1975 Number	Change 1960-1975 Percent	1981	Change 1975-1981 Number	Change 1975-1981 Percent
Northeast Region	1,936.5	3,225.7	1,289.2	66.6	3,420.9	195.2	6.1
Middle Atlantic Division	1,478.4	1,470.8	992.4	67.1	2,585.1	114.3	4.6
New England Division	458.1	754.9	296.8	64.8	835.8	80.9	10.7
North Central Region	2,199.4	3,700.8	1,501.4	68.3	4,072.6	371.8	10.0
East North Central Division	1,479.1	2,503.5	1,024.4	69.3	2,768.3	264.8	10.6
West North Central Division	720.3	1,197.3	477.0	66.2	1,304.3	107.0	8.9
South Region	2,620.1	4,918.1	2,298.0	87.7	5,940.6	1,022.5	20.8
South Atlantic Division	1,347.1	2,662.2	1,315.1	97.6	3,128.3	466.1	17.5
East South Central Division	497.3	864.6	367.3	73.9	1,057.4	192.8	22.3
West South Central Division	775.7	1,391.3	615.5	79.4	1,754.9	363.6	26.1
West Region	1,533.4	2,922.7	1,389.6	90.6	3,297.4	374.7	12.8
Mountain Division	403.1	806.2	406.1	100.0	956.3	150.1	18.6
Pacific Division	1,130.3	2,116.5	986.2	87.3	2,341.1	224.6	10.6
U.S. Total[2]	8,289.4	14,767.3	6,477.9	78.1	16,731.5	1,964.2	13.3

Notes: [1]Employees on nonagriculture payrolls as of March of the respective years.
[2]Excludes Hawaii and Alaska.

Source: U.S. Department of Labor, Bureau of Labor Statistics, *Employment and Earnings* (Washington, D.C.: U.S. Government Printing Office, Monthly).

EXHIBIT 77

Regional Growth Shares of Government Employment Change: 1960-1981[1]

(Numbers in Thousands)

	Absolute Growth Increment				Percentage Share of National Growth			
Region and Division	**1960-1965**	**1965-1970**	**1970-1975**	**1975-1981**	**1960-1965**	**1965-1970**	**1970-1975**	**1975-1981**
Northeast Region	323.2	565.3	400.7	195.2	20.5	19.5	19.8	9.9
Middle Atlantic Division	256.9	457.0	278.5	114.3	16.3	15.8	13.7	5.8
New England Division	66.3	108.3	122.2	80.9	4.2	3.7	6.0	4.1
North Central Region	377.5	800.8	323.1	371.8	24.0	27.7	15.9	18.9
East Central Division	256.0	574.7	193.7	264.8	16.2	19.9	9.5	13.5
West North Central Division	121.5	226.1	129.4	107.0	7.7	7.8	6.4	5.4
South Region	517.3	932.7	848.0	1,022.5	32.9	32.3	41.9	52.1
South Atlantic Division	277.4	533.4	504.3	466.1	17.6	18.4	24.9	23.7
East South Central Division	101.6	138.1	127.6	192.8	6.4	4.7	6.3	9.8
West South Central Division	138.3	261.2	216.1	363.6	8.8	9.0	10.7	18.5
West Region	353.2	588.5	447.6	374.7	22.4	20.3	22.1	19.1
Mountain Division	88.0	157.0	158.1	150.1	5.6	5.4	7.8	7.6
Pacific Division	265.2	431.5	289.5	224.6	16.8	14.9	14.3	11.4
U.S. Total[2]	1,571.2	2,887.3	2,019.4	1,964.2	100.0	100.0	100.0	100.0

Notes: [1]Employees on nonagriculture payrolls as of March of the respective periods.
[2]Excludes Hawaii and Alaska.

Source: U.S. Department of Labor, Bureau of Labor Statistics, *Employment and Earnings* (Washington, D.C.: U.S. Government Printing Office, Monthly).

and also of population increments. Whether it is a field office of the FHA, of the Veteran's Administation, or of the Social Security office, they are all in the business of servicing local activity and will increase or decrease in proportion to local employment and population gains. To that degree government employment, rather than being independent of other forms of growth, is in large part its natural concomitant. Thus government employment mirrors the realities of demographic shifts and the geographic movement of other economic sectors.

SUMMARY

The regional patterns of population growth are closely paralleled by concurrent regional employment shifts. As is the case with other allied demographic and economic phenomena reviewed in this study, the direction of causation is not clear-cut. But the regional population and employment linkage has emerged as a major dynamic of America in the 1980s.

1. Analysis of long-term employment patterns provides statistical evidence of a secular relative diminishment of the economic posture of the Northeast and North Central regions, and a substantial relative and absolute enhancement of the South and West.
2. National economic cycles have exacerbated regional growth differentials. When national employment growth slows, the Northeast and North Central regions bear the brunt of the slowdown. When the economy advances more rapidly, the major benefits accrue to the South and West.
3. The sharpest variations are evident in the manufacturing sector. The aging industrial belt is afflicted with a critical mass of shrinking old-line manufacturing activity. The overwhelming bulk of new manufacturing jobs has been secured by the Sunbelt.
4. Population- and economic-serving activities are encompassed by the private nonmanufacturing and governmental sectors. These rapid growth elements (particularly nonmanufacturing) again have largely settled in the southern and western sectors of the nation.
5. Demographic mobility was such throughout the 1970s as to facilitate the regional spatial redistribution of the nation's economic activity, i.e., people were able to follow jobs (or conversely, population movements stimulated employment growth). In the 1980s, however, housing and economic constraints may impede demographic mobility, exacerbating the strains caused by inter-regional job-growth variations.
6. Partially obscured by the employment boom of the late 1970s, the tendency of the national economy toward stagnation in the early 1980s may evoke the regional trauma that surfaced during the 1974-1975 recession. The capacity of the economy to adapt to world economic strictures will be mirrored in the nation's inter-regional employment gaps.

Chapter Twelve

POPULATION DISTRIBUTION: METROPOLITAN, NONMETROPOLITAN, AND INTRAMETROPOLITAN

The basic challenge of contemporary planning activity has been set within the framework of the decline of the central city and the resynthesis of the mainstream of American life in suburbia. The intrametropolitan struggles associated with racial resegregation, fiscal shortfall, infrastructure duplication, and environmental impact are just beginning to become aware of a broader change of encompassing significance: the very role of the historic industrial metropolis may soon be coming into question. Our areal concerns have lagged behind reality; the focus was on the good will of City Hall toward slum neighborhoods while the city as a whole faltered. We talked of metropolitan government while exurbia boomed and regional shifts dominated the scene. The drive toward a revitalized economy now must take cognizance of world competition. Left behind are many of the old growth nodes of the past.

METROPOLITAN-NONMETROPOLITAN TENSIONS

For the past half century, the major growth poles of American society were its metropolitan centers. Yet this convention has been relegated to the annals of urban history. As shown in Exhibit 78, large metropolitan agglomerations (as defined in 1981) experienced the final stages of their service as the nation's dominant growth loci during the 1960-to-1970 era.[24] Their average annual population increase (1.7 percent) exceeded that of the United States (1.3 percent), and far outdistanced nonmetropolitan territories (-0.2 percent)

The threshold changes that have occurred since 1970 are substantial. From 1970 to 1980, large metropolitan areas have been transformed into settings of slow growth, evidencing an average annual rate of population increase of 0.6

EXHIBIT 78

Metropolitan and Nonmetropolitan Population Change: 1960 to 1980

(Numbers in Thousands)

Metropolitan Status[1]	1960[2]	1970	1980	Average Annual Percent Change 1960-1970	Average Annual Percent Change 1970-1980
Total Metropolitan	128,841	153,694	169,405	1.8	1.0
Large Metropolitan	68,239	80,793	85,442	1.7	0.6
Other Metropolitan	60,602	72,901	83,963	1.9	1.4
Nonmetropolitan	50,470	49,608	57,100	-0.2	1.4
Total United States	179,311	203,302	226,505	1.3	1.1

Notes: [1]"Large metropolitan" includes areas identified individually in Exhibit 81. Metropolitan areas as defined in 1981 — 318 SMSAs (excluding 5 in Puerto Rico).

[2]Data for "other metropolitan" and "nonmetropolitan" for 1960 not strictly comparable to 1970 and 1980 data.

Sources: U.S. Bureau of the Census, Current Population Reports, Series P-20, No. 363, *Population Profile of the United States: 1980,* U.S. Government Printing Office, Washington, D.C., 1981; and U.S. Bureau of the Census, 1980 Census of Population, *Supplementary Reports,* "Standard Metropolitan Statistical Areas and Standard Consolidated Statistical Areas: 1980," PC80-S1-5, U.S. Government Printing Office, Washington, D.C., 1981.

percent. At the same time, smaller (other) metropolitan areas experienced growth rates of 1.4 percent. Yet the latter are being challenged by the revolutionary surge of nonmetropolitan growth, where population increases also averaged 1.4 percent annually. In an equally telling transformation detailed in Exhibit 79, metropolitan areas with 1 million or more persons (as defined in 1979) experienced a net outmigration of 1.4 million people, while nonmetropolitan territories had a net inmigration of 2.7 million over the 1970 to 1978 period. (The 1978 terminal point is still the latest date for metropolitan-nonmetropolitan components of change tabulations.) Some of this shift undoubtedly signifies the drive toward exurbia and can be attributed to the lagging pace of metropolitan definition. However, the latter may be only a secondary explanation for the phenomenon.

The pattern is clarified in Exhibit 80, which partitions metropolitan and nonmetropolitan population growth patterns by regional location from 1960 to 1980. It is the large metropolitan complexes of the Northeast that dominate the post-1970 experience of metropolitan decline. Also exhibiting similar

EXHIBIT 79

Metropolitan and Nonmetropolitan Population and Components of Change: 1970 to 1978[1]

(Numbers in Thousands)

	Population		Change: 1970-1978		Components of Change 1970-1978	
Metropolitan Status	**1970**	**1978**	**Number**	**Percent**	**Natural Increase**	**Net Migration**
Total Metropolitan	150,684	160,040	9,356	6.2	8,624	732
Areas with 1 million or more population	85,252	88,216	2,963	3.5	4,325	-1,362
Areas with less than 1 million population	65,432	61,824	6,392	9.8	4,299	2,093
Nonmetropolitan	52,618	58,023	5,405	10.3	2,695	2,710
Total United States	203,302	218,063	14,761	7.3	71,319	3,442

Notes: [1]Metropolitan areas as defined June 30, 1979. Metropolitan-nonmetropolitan data in this exhibit are *not* strictly comparable to data in Exhibits 78, 80, 81 or 82.

Source: U.S. Bureau of the Census, Current Population Reports, Series P-25, No. 873, *Estimates of the Population of Counties and Metropolitan Areas: July 1, 1977 and 1978,* U.S. Government Printing Office, Washington, D.C., 1980.

EXHIBIT 80

Population by Regions and Metropolitan Status: 1960 to 1980[1]

(Numbers in Thousands)

Region	Population 1960[2]	1970	1980
Northeast			
Large Metropolitan	26,027	28,590	27,381
Other Metropolitan	12,582	13,957	14,360
Nonmetropolitan	6,069	6,514	7,395
North Central			
Large Metropolitan	18,858	21,384	21,449
Other Metropolitan	16,615	19,245	20,258
Nonmetropolitan	16,146	15,962	17,147
South			
Large Metropolitan	9,648	13,012	15,980
Other Metropolitan	23,160	28,457	34,373
Nonmetropolitan	22,153	21,344	24,997
West			
Large Metropolitan	13,706	17,807	20,632
Other Metropolitan	8,245	11,242	14,972
Nonmetropolitan	6,102	5,789	7,561

Notes: [1]"Large metropolitan" includes areas identified individually in Exibit 81. Metropolitan areas as defined in 1981 - 318 SMSAs (excluding 5 in Puerto Rico).

[2]Data for "other metropolitan" and "nonmetropolitan" for 1960 not strictly comparable to 1970 and 1980 data.

Sources: U.S. Bureau of the Census, Current Population Reports, Series P-20, No. 363, *Population Profile of the United States: 1980,* U.S. Government Printing Office, Washington, D.C., 1981; and U.S. Bureau of the Census, 1980 Census of Population, *Supplementary Reports,* "Standard Metropolitan Statistical Areas and Standard Consolidated Statistical Areas: 1980," PC80-S1-5, U.S. Government Printing Office, Washington, D.C., 1981.

symptoms, although not yet shrinking, are their equivalents in the North Central states. In sharp contrast is the status of large metropolitan areas in the South and West, which demonstrated a sustained pattern of growth through the decade of the 1970s.

The major focal points of growth in the Northeast and North Central states are nonmetropolitan areas, which exceeded even the positive growth performances of the smaller (other) metropolitan areas. In the South and West, the largest increments of population growth on an absolute basis accrued to small metropolitan settings. The linkage of regional and metropolitan growth patterns becomes apparent when it is realized that the Northeast has nearly three-fifths of its total population concentrated in four large metropolitan areas. The virtual national halt in large metropolitan growth has therefore a much greater effect in the Northeast than the South, where only one-fifth of the population resides in large metropolitan settings. Similarly, the revitalization of the nonmetropolitan sector has negligible positive effects in the Northeast, where only one-seventh of the population is nonmetropolitan; in contrast, the South, where one-third of the population so resides, experiences much greater repercussions from nonmetropolitan growth.

The South has the advantage of maturing late, the older areas of the country are frozen in the patterns of yesteryear. Avoiding the question of which shift — regional or metropolitan — is the primary causal factor, we can be certain that their interlinkage is forging a critical dynamic for the immediate future.

When the data for the twenty largest metropolitan agglomerations (as defined in 1981) are further dissected, their losses appear more alarming. As shown in Exhibit 81, seven out of ten major metropolises in the Northeast and North Central regions experienced population losses from 1970 to 1980. Yet in the South, only Washington, D.C., and Baltimore reflect slow growth; more than compensating for the latter's performance has been the phenomenal growth of Houston, Miami, Atlanta, and Dallas, clearly indexed by decade growth rates exceeding 25 percent.

As expected, the West exhibits a pattern similar to the South. Indeed, the San Diego SMSA experienced a growth rate of 37.1 percent, partially reflecting its attractiveness as a magnet for military retirees.

And the rates of population decline of the older regions' metropolises are far from trivial. In New York, for example, 5.4 percent of its 1970 population was lost, with similar rates afflicting the Pittsburgh (-5.7 percent) and Cleveland (-5.5 percent) metropolitan areas. Even the non-declining metropolitan areas of the Northeast and North Central states (excluding Minneapolis-St. Paul) are growing at a rate far slower than all of the Southern and Western metropolises.

Historically, the sheer growth in population, particularly through migration, generated much of the social and economic stress of our older urban centers. This pattern has changed very markedly, providing both hope and new challenge. The problems of coping with increased housing demand, of overcrowded schools and overstressed physical facilities may be somewhat alleviated by the new conditions of population stability and decline; but in their place is the question of the fiscal balance — of the economic wherewithal within the older metropolitan settings with which to service the remaining population. These questions take on even more significance as equally important and distressing patterns of change surface inside of metropolitan areas.

EXHIBIT 81

Population for the Twenty Largest Metropolitan Agglomerations[1]: 1960 to 1980

(Numbers in Thousands)

Region and Area	Population 1960	1970	1980	Change: 1960-1970 Number	Percent	Change: 1970-1980 Number	Percent
Northeast Region							
New York SCSA	15,405	17,035	16,120	1,630	10.6	-915	-5.4
Philadelphia SCSA	5,024	5,628	5,549	604	12.0	-79	-1.4
Boston SCSA	3,193	3,526	3,448	333	10.4	-78	-2.2
Pittsburgh SMSA	2,405	2,401	2,264	-4	-0.2	-137	-5.7
North Central							
Chicago SCSA	6,794	7,726	7,868	932	13.7	142	1.8
Detroit SCSA	4,122	4,669	4,618	547	13.3	-51	-1.1
Cleveland SCSA	2,732	3,000	2,834	268	9.8	-166	-5.5
St. Louis SMSA	2,144	2,411	2,355	267	12.5	-56	-2.3
Minneapolis-St. Paul SMSA	1,598	1,965	2,144	367	23.0	149	7.6
Cincinnati SCSA	1,468	1,613	1,660	145	9.9	47	2.9

EXHIBIT 81 (Continued)
Population for the Twenty Largest Metropolitan Agglomerations[1]: 1960 to 1980
(Numbers in Thousands)

	Population			Change: 1960-1970		Change: 1970-1980	
Region and Area	**1960**	**1970**	**1980**	**Number**	**Percent**	**Number**	**Percent**
South Region							
Washington, D.C. SMSA	2,097	2,910	3,060	813	38.8	150	5.2
Dallas-Ft. Worth SMSA	1,738	2,378	2,975	640	36.8	597	25.1
Houston SCSA	1,571	2,169	3,101	598	38.1	932	43.0
Miami SCSA	1,269	1,888	2,640	619	48.8	752	39.8
Baltimore SMSA	1,804	2,071	2,174	267	14.8	103	5.0
Atlanta SMSA	1,169	1,596	2,030	427	36.5	434	27.2
West Region							
Los Angeles SCSA	7,752	9,981	11,496	2,229	28.8	1,515	15.2
San Francisco SCSA	3,492	4,631	5,182	1,139	32.6	551	11.9
Seattle SCSA	1,429	1,837	2,092	408	28.6	255	13.9
San Diego SMSA	1,033	1,358	1,862	325	31.5	504	37.1

Note: [1]Standard consolidated statistical areas (SCSAs) and standard metropolitan statistical areas (SMSAs) defined by Office of Management and Budget as of June 30, 1981.

Sources: U.S. Bureau of the Census, *Commerce News,* "Major Metropolitan Complexes Show Slower Overall Population Growth During 1970s, 1980 Census Analysis Reveals," CB81-61, Public Information Office, Washington, D.C., April 8, 1981; and U.S. Bureau of the Census, 1980 Census of Population, *Supplementary Reports,* "Standard Metropolitan Statistical Areas and Standard Consolidated Statistical Areas: 1980," PC80-S1-5, U.S. Government Printing Office, Washington, D.C., 1981.

INTRA-METROPOLITAN SHIFTS

The history of America's major cities is one of meeting — and surmounting — the problems of growth and change. But for the first time, the nation's central cities in total are losing population, and doing so quite markedly, while the corresponding suburban rings expanded considerably (Exhibit 82). Indeed, while nonmetropolitan growth rates have moved past those of formally defined metropolitan areas (as defined in 1970), the suburban rings still represent the fastest-growing territories of America, although being pressed hard by nonmetropolitan areas.

EXHIBIT 82

Noninstitutional Population, Metropolitan and Intrametropolitan Status, 1970 to 1979, U.S. Total

(Numbers in Millions)

	1970	1979	Average Annual Percent Change
Total SMSAs	137.1	145.4	0.7%
Central Cities	62.9	60.6	-0.4
Outside Central Cities	74.2	84.8	1.5
Nonmetropolitan Areas	62.8	69.9	1.2

Notes: Covers 243 SMSAs as defined in 1970 census publications, therefore not directly comparable to preceding exhibits in definition. Limited to noninstitutional population.

Source: U.S. Bureau of the Census, Bureau of the Census, *Current Population Reports,* Series P-20, No. 350.

But the latter pattern does not strictly hold for the nation's large, aging metropolitan areas in the Northeast and North Central regions. As detailed in Exhibit 83, the large central cities of the "Frostbelt," while afflicted with substantial population losses, often fail to account for all of the decline of their metropolitan areas. For example, between 1970 and 1980, New York City and Pittsburgh lost 825,000 and 96,000 people, respectively (Exhibit 83). However, the New York metropolitan area lost 915,000 people while the Pittsburgh SMSA lost 137,000 (Exhibit 81), totals in excess of their central city losses. Thus, suburban decline is beginning to appear in select metropolitan settings (although the presence of smaller, aging sub-cities within this context plays a significant role).

The actual magnitude of select central city declines is remarkable when viewed over a longer time frame (Exhibit 83). From 1950 to 1980, St. Louis lost 47 percent of its population, Buffalo 38 percent, and Pittsburgh and Cleveland 37 percent — with the largest proportion of the declines attributable to the 1970-to-1980 period.

EXHIBIT 83
Population Change, Selected Cities
1950 to 1980

City	1950[1]	1970[2]	1980[3]	Change: 1950-1980 Number	Change: 1950-1980 Percent	Change: 1970-1980 Number	Change: 1970-1980 Percent
Boston	801,444	641,071	562,994	-238,450	-29.8	-78,077	-12.2
Buffalo	580,132	462,768	357,870	-222,262	-38.3	-104,898	-22.7
Chicago	3,620,962	3,369,357	3,005,072	-615,890	-17.0	-364,285	-10.8
Cincinnati	503,998	453,514	385,457	-118,541	-23.5	-68,057	-15.0
Cleveland	914,808	750,879	573,822	-340,986	-37.3	-177,057	-23.6
Detroit	1,849,568	1,514,063	1,203,339	-646,229	-34.9	-310,724	-20.5
Minneapolis	521,718	434,400	370,951	-150,767	-28.9	-63,449	-14.6
New York City	7,891,957	7,895,563	7,071,030	-820,927	-10.4	-824,553	-10.4
Newark	438,776	381,930	329,248	-109,528	-25.0	-52,682	-13.8
Philadelphia	2,071,605	1,949,996	1,688,210	-383,395	-18.5	-261,786	-13.4
Pittsburgh	676,806	520,089	423,938	-252,868	-37.4	-96,151	-18.5
St. Louis	856,796	622,236	453,085	-403,711	-47.1	-169,151	-27.2

Notes: [1]April 1, 1950 Census.
[2]April 1, 1970 Census.
[3]April 1, 1980 Census.

Sources: U.S. Bureau of the Census, *County and City Data Book, 1956* (A Statistical Abstract Supplement), U.S. Government Printing Office, Washington, D.C., 1957; and U.S. Bureau of the Census, *Commerce News,* "Three Cities of 100,000 or More At Least Doubled Population Between 1970 and 1980, Census Bureau Reports," CB81-92, Public Information Office, Washington, D.C., June 3, 1981.

As hypothesized earlier, the emerging household formations of America are of a format that are at least susceptible to having urban preferences, i.e., a diminished necessity for securing ideal child-rearing environments. And the gap between income potentials and shelter costs (chapter 9) also suggests a potential greater utilization of central-city housing inventories. But whatever tentative stirrings exist for a back-to-the-city movement must be tempered by the sheer magnitude of the declines documented in Exhibit 83.

SUMMARY

The post-1970 era requires a new basic reference framework not only to account for an increasing regional presence, but also to recognize the emergence of nonmetropolitan places as major growth loci. Nowhere are the conventions of the past more sternly challenged than in the new experience of declining metropolitan areas.

1. From 1970 to 1980, metropolitan areas in total (318 SMSAs) experienced an average annual growth rate of 1.0 percent. In contrast, nonmetropolitan areas had a 1.4 percent annual average increase in population, a reversal of what had long been considered the conventional relationship.
2. It is the large metropolitan agglomerations of the Northeast and North Central regions that led this reversal, with most experiencing absolute population declines over the 1970 to 1980 period. The future role of the traditional industrial metropolis is increasingly coming into question.
3. Similarly, America's central cities in total for the first time lost population, and did so quite markedly.
4. As a result, America's largest central cities have experienced an acceleration of their rate of population loss within the past 30 years. By 1980, St. Louis, for example, saw its 1950 population level decline by 47.1 percent, Pittsburgh by 37.4 percent, Cleveland by 37.3 percent, and Buffalo by 38.3 percent.
5. The implications of these shifts are manifold. To cite but one example, the problem of the central city may no longer be adding to the housing stock, but rather the provision of removal mechanisms for those units no longer required by a shrinking population. While the issue may be offset temporarily by continued contraction in household sizes, to view such problems as residential abandonment in the abstract without studying the broader population shifts is to do them less than justice.

   The stagnation of post-1973 income levels was offset by personal capital-asset growth for homeowning Americans. This encouraged mobility — both for jobseekers and retirees. Will the faltering of this accumulative effect slow migration? Or will the forces that became evident in the 1970s continue to dominate the decade? Certainly the flywheels of plant modernity, industry mix, and right-to-work laws — to say nothing of comparative youth and fertility in the newer areas of the country — strongly suggest continuity, even if temporarily slowed by recession.

The challenge of growth, however, must be viewed within an international context — with subsections of the country increasingly the prisoners of national success — or failure. The 1970s are slipping away into history but the incredible achievement of the United States in absorbing an unprecedented explosion of the labor force should not be underestimated.

As the society girds up for reindustrialization, if at the cost of redistribution, it does so with a more mature, experienced demographic base. The awesome dependency ratios of the past — of children — will be followed by those of age in the future. But the decade of the 1980s is one of potential balance that can and must provide support for solid development.

The "ease" of riding the baby boom may be over, the challenges of a diversified society are not trivial — but neither were the barriers that have been successfully surmounted in the past.

Appendix A

RESTRUCTURED EMPLOYMENT SECTORS

This appendix provides the precise composition of the employment categories defined in Exhibit 40 (chapter 6). They are proximately based on the *Business Week* (June 1, 1981) segments designed to conceptualize the American economy as five distinct sectors. The totals differ from those of chapter 11 because of two definitional variations: the regional tabulations and U.S. totals in chapter 11 exclude Hawaii and Alaska; and the wholesale and retail trade sector is excluded from the tabulations of this appendix, as well as from Exhibit 40, chapter 6.

The general *Business Week* hypothesis is that the American economy is beset by centrifugal forces, which are restructuring the economy into five distinct and separate sectors — old-line industry, high technology, energy, services, and agriculture. These individual subeconomies no longer act as a whole; thus older conventional partitions may not be adequate to address this emerging segmentation.

EXHIBIT A-1
Restructured Employment Sectors,[1]
U.S. Total: 1976 to 1981
(Numbers in Thousands)

			Change: 1976 to 1981	
Sector	**1976**	**1981**	**Number**	**Percent**
Old Line Industry	11,574.3	20,306.4	1,758.6	9.5%
High Technology	3,074.3	4,075.4	1,001.1	32.6
Energy	757.7	1,084.9	327.2	43.2
Services	26,354.2	33,288.3	6,934.1	26.3
Government	15,322.0	16,408.0	1,086.0	7.1

Notes: [1]Nonfarm payroll employment as of March of the respective years; includes Hawaii and Alaska; excludes wholesale and retail trade.

Source: U.S. Department of Labor, Bureau of Labor Statistics, *Employment and Earnings*, Monthly.

EXHIBIT A-2

Old Line Industry Composition[1]
U.S. Total: 1976 to 1981
(Numbers in Thousands)

			Change: 1976 to 1981	
Sector	**1976**	**1981**	**Number**	**Percent**
Metal Mining	89.6	101.5	11.9	13.3
Nonmet. Minerals	110.0	107.5	-2.5	-2.3
Construction	3,103.0	4,135.0	1,032.0	33.3
Lumber & Wood Prod.	578.9	671.4	92.5	16.0
Furni. & Fixtures	483.4	477.5	-5.9	-1.2
Stone, Clay & Glass	602.9	641.3	38.4	6.4
Prim. Metals Indus.	1,169.4	1,129.1	-40.3	-3.4
Fabric. Metal Prod.	1,364.5	1,603.9	239.4	17.5
Machinery	1,769.2	2,058.0	288.8	16.3
Transp. Equip.	1,217.1	1,093.0	-124.1	-10.2
Misc. Mfg. Indus.	414.6	409.7	-4.9	-1.2
Food & Kindred Prod.	1,626.9	1,609.7	-17.2	-1.1
Tobacco Manu.	70.3	67.9	-2.4	-3.4
Textile Mill Prod.	962.9	853.0	-109.9	-11.4
Apparel & Other Tex.	1,322.9	1,299.8	-23.1	-1.7
Paper & Allied Prod.	665.5	688.5	23.0	3.5
Printing & Publshg.	1,072.7	1,291.4	218.7	20.4
Chemicals & Allied Prod.	1,026.9	1,113.2	86.3	8.4
Rubber & Misc. Plastics	622.1	714.1	92.0	14.8
Leather & Leather Prod.	275.0	240.9	-34.1	-12.4
TOTAL	18,547.8	20,306.4	1,758.6	9.5

Notes: [1]Nonfarm payroll employment as of March of the respective years; includes Hawaii and Alaska; excludes wholesale and retail trade.

Source: U.S. Department of Labor, Bureau of Labor Statistics, *Employment and Earnings,* Monthly.

EXHIBIT A-3
High Technology and Energy Composition,[1] U.S. Total: 1976 to 1981
(Numbers in Thousands)

	High Technology		Change: 1976 to 1981	
Industry	**1976**	**1981**	**Number**	**Percent**
Offices & Computing Machines	283.4	446.0	162.6	57.4
Electric and Electronic Equipment	1,799.4	2,146.0	346.6	19.3
Aircraft & Parts	490.1	665.4	175.5	35.8
Guided Missles, Space Vehicles[2]	—	118.5	—	—
Instrument & Related Products	501.4	699.5	198.1	39.5
TOTAL	3,074.3	4,075.4	1,001.1	32.6
	Energy			
Coal Mining	213.3	270.1	56.8	26.6
Oil & Gas Extraction	345.7	606.7	261.0	75.5
Petroleum & Coal Products	198.7	208.1	9.4	4.7
TOTAL	757.7	1,084.9	327.2	43.2

Notes: [1]Nonfarm payroll employment as of March of the respective years; includes Hawaii and Alaska; excludes wholesale and retail trade.
[2]Encompassed in other categories of this group in 1976.

Source: U.S. Department of Labor, Bureau of Labor Statistics, *Employment and Earnings*, Monthly.

EXHIBIT A-4
Services and Government Composition,[1]
U.S. Total: 1976 to 1981
(Numbers in Thousands)

	Services		Change: 1976 to 1981	
Industry	**1976**	**1981**	**Number**	**Percent**
Transp. & Public Utilities	4,462.0	5,107.0	645.0	14.5
Eating & Drinking Places	3,339.2	4,826.3	1,487.1	44.5
Finance, Ins. & Real Est.	4,246.0	5,252.0	1,006.0	23.7
Services	14,307.0	18,103.0	3,796.0	26.5
TOTAL	26,354.2	33,288.3	6,934.1	26.3
	Government			
Federal	2,724.0	2,769.0	45.0	1.7
State	3,353.3	3,652.2	298.9	8.9
Local	9,244.5	9,986.9	742.4	8.0
TOTAL	15,332.0	16,408.0	1,086.0	7.1

Notes: [1]Nonfarm payroll employment as of March of the respective years; includes Hawaii and Alaska; excludes wholesale and retail trade.
[2]Encompassed in other categories of this group in 1976.

Source: U.S. Department of Labor, Bureau of Labor Statistics, *Employment and Earnings,* Monthly.

Appendix B

EXHIBIT B-1

Total Employment: United States,
West Germany and Japan - 1969 to 1979
(Numbers in Thousands)

				Change: 1969 to 1979	
	1969	**1974**	**1979**	**Number**	**Percent**
United States	77,902	85,936	96,945	19,043	24.4%
West Germany	25,871	25,688	25,041	-830	-3.2
Japan	50,400	52,370	54,790	4,390	8.7

Note: Annual averages; totals include wage and salary employees, self-employed persons and unpaid family workers.

Source: OECD (Organization for Economic Cooperation and Development), *Labor Force Statistics, 1968-1979.* Paris, 1981.

EXHIBIT B-2

Comparative Employment Change by Industrial Sector
United States, West Germany and Japan: 1969-1979
(Numbers in Thousands)

	United States				West Germany				Japan			
			Change: 1969-1979				Change: 1969-1979				Change: 1969-1979	
	1969	1979	Number	Percent	1969	1979	Number	Percent	1969	1979	Number	Percent
TOTAL	77,902	96,945	19,043	24.4%	25,871	25,041	-830	-3.2%	50,400	54,790	4,390	8.7%
Agriculture, Hunting, Forestry, and Fishing	3,698	3,455	-243	-6.6	2,395	1,558	-837	-34.9	9,460	6,130	-3,330	-35.2
Manufacturing, Mining and Quarrying	21,780	23,001	1,221	5.6	10,407	9,122	-1,285	-12.3	13,690	13,450	-240	-1.8
Utilities	933	1,101	168	18.0	193	220	27	14.0	270	330	60	22.2
Construction	4,820	6,299	1,479	30.7	2,066	1,891	-175	-8.5	3,710	5,360	1,650	44.5
Wholesale and Retail Trade, and Hotels and Restaurants	15,418	20,769	5,351	34.7	3,831	3,617	-214	-5.6	10,010	12,280	2,270	22.7
Transportation, Storage and Communications	4,713	5,576	863	18.3	1,476	1,493	17	1.2	3,110	3,490	380	12.2
Finance, Insurance, Real Estate and Business Services	5,093	7,979	2,886	56.7	1,060	1,369	309	29.2	1,320	1,850	530	40.2
Community, Social and Personal Services	21,447	28,764	7,317	34.1	4,443	5,771	1,328	29.9	8,780	11,810	3,030	34.5
Other	—	—	—	—	—	—	—	—	50	90	40	80.0

Note: Annual averages; totals include wage and salary employees, self-employed persons, and unpaid family workers.

Source: OECD (Organization for Economic Cooperation and Development), *Labor Force Statistics, 1968-1979.* Paris, 1981.

EXHIBIT B-3

Comparative Employment Structures
United States, West Germany and Japan: 1969-1979
(Percent Distribution)

	United States		West Germany		Japan	
	1969	**1979**	**1969**	**1979**	**1969**	**1979**
TOTAL	100.0%	100.0%	100.0%	100.0%	100.0%	100.0%
Agriculture, Hunting, Forestry, and Fishing	4.7	3.6	9.3	6.2	18.8	11.2
Manufacturing, Mining and Quarrying	28.0	23.7	40.2	36.4	27.2	24.5
Utilities	1.2	1.1	0.7	0.9	0.5	0.6
Construction	6.2	6.5	8.0	7.6	7.4	9.8
Wholesale and Retail Trade, and Hotels and Restaurants	19.8	21.4	14.8	14.4	19.9	22.4
Transportation, Storage and Communication	6.0	5.8	5.7	6.0	6.2	6.4
Finance, Insurance, Real Estate and Business Services	6.5	8.2	4.1	5.5	2.6	3.4
Community, Social and Personal Services	27.5	29.7	17.2	23.0	17.4	21.6
Other	—	—	—	—	0.1	0.2

Note: May not add due to rounding.

Source: OECD (Organization for Economic Cooperation and Development), *Labor Force Statistics, 1968-1979*. Paris, 1981.

NOTES

1. "While the total population has increased throughout American history, the rate of growth has undergone a long-term decline with the only major interruption being due to the 'baby boom' following the Second World War. During the first half of the 19th century, the population of the United States increased at an average rate of about 3 percent per year. Subsequently, the growth rate dropped, largely because of a pronounced decline in fertility, to an average of 0.7 percent per year during the 1930s. The annual growth rate then increased to 1.7 percent during the 1950s at the peak of the baby boom before declining again to the current level, which is about equal to the historically low rate of the 1930s." U.S. Bureau of the Census, *Current Population Reports*, Series P-25, no. 704, "Projections of the Population of the United States: 1977 to 2050" (Washington, D.C.: U.S. Government Printing Office, July 1977), pp. 4-5.
2. The reader is cautioned on the July 1 benchmark of the data of Exhibit 2. Since projection and estimation dates vary from the traditional April 1 base of the decennial census, care should be exercised in any tabular comparisons. July 1 usually marks the beginning of the estimation and projection periods.
   Caution is also advised in regard to any comparison of Exhibit 2 to previously published annual estimates. The final 1980 census count of total resident population totaled 226.5 million people (April 1); the original 1980 estimate (Jan. 1) totaled 221.2 million people. It is this differential which had to be allocated to previously published estimates. See Notes 3, 5, 6 and 7.
3. Preliminary to the 1980 Census, estimates for 1971 through 1980 were based on the 1970 Census count and administrative records—statistics on births and deaths provided by the National Center for Health Statistics, statistics on immigration provided by the Immigration and Naturalization Service of the Department of Justice, as well as Department of Defense records. With the availability of the 1980 census counts, estimates previously established for intercensus years were adjusted by distributing the error of closure (the difference between the 1980 census count and the post-census estimate for April 1, 1980) in proportion to time elapsed and population size. See U.S. Department of Commerce, Bureau of the Census, *Current Population Reports*, Series P-25, no. 899, "Estimates of the Population of the United States to March 1, 1981."
4. There are a number of measures that gauge the role of births in population change (natility) and/or actual birth performance (fertility). The following is a highly simplified presentation of the basic indicators, secured from the Census Bureau's, *The Methods and Materials of Demography*. (Full citation at end of note.)

The simplest and most common measure of fertility is the *total* or *crude birth rate*, defined as the number of births occurring in a year per 1,000 midyear population, that is:

$$\frac{B}{P} \times 1000$$

This measure is used in chapter 3 to describe the long-term secular pattern of birth rates and to establish international comparisons. It is useful in indicating directly the influence of natility to the overall population growth rate; however, it is limited analytically because it is influenced by the specific age-sex composition of a population, i.e., the total birth rate may rise or fall simply as a function of the changing size of the child-bearing age cohorts, for example.

Age-specific birth rates are also commonly employed. An age specific birth rate is defined as the number of births to women of a given age group per 1,000 women in that age group. For example, the rate attendant to 20 to 24 years of age women is:

$$\frac{B_{20\text{-}24}}{P^{f}_{20\text{-}24}} \times 1000$$

This measure thus is unaffected by age structure variation, and is useful, for example, in elaborating long-term trends or cross-sectional comparisons.

Another overall age-limited measure is the *general fertility rate*, defined as the number of births per 1,000 women of child-bearing age. Typically, the total number of births is employed in the numerator and the female population 15 to 44 years of age in the denominator:

$$\frac{B}{P^{f}_{15\text{-}44}} \times 1000$$

The *total fertility* rate is the sum of the age-specific birth rates of women over their reproductive span, as observed in a given year. Hence, it is an age-sex adjusted measure of fertility that takes account of age detail within the childbearing ages. It is defined as:

$$X = \sum_{15}^{44} \frac{B_x}{P_x} \times 1000$$

The total fertility rate gives the number of births 1,000 women would have if they experienced a given set of age-specific birth rates throughout their reproductive span. It can also be interpreted as representing the completed fertility of a synthetic cohort of women. See: U.S. Bureau of the Census, *The Methods and Materials of Demography* by Henry S. Shryock, Jacob S. Siegel, and Associates, 3rd printing (rev.) U.S. Government Printing Office (Washington, D.C.: 1975).

5. The components of population change — net natural increase and net migration — are determined by administrative records (see note 3). The sum of net natural increase and migration should equal the absolute annual population increments detailed in Exhibit 2. However, they do *not*. In eliminating the error of closure with the 1980 census count, the total annual increments were adjusted, but the components were not. This inconsistency has not, as of this writing, been rectified. The present assumption is that the difference reflects the more complete coverage of the 1980 census as compared to the 1970 census.
6. The total population-growth data in Exhibit 5 for the United States are estimates that have not been adjusted to the 1980 census. Hence they differ from the estimates of Exhibit 2, and underestimate the actual growth increment.
7. A note of caution must be raised in viewing the projections presented in Exhibit 6. Since the latest Census Bureau projections were undertaken before the 1980 census, the baseline (or starting point) now appears low, rendering each of the projection sets smaller in magnitude than would be the case if a post-1980 census calibrated baseline were employed.
8. The Census Bureau considers the Series II projection to be its best estimate, with the assumed level of future fertility corresponding closely to that suggested by recent survey data. The fertility assumptions of Series I and Series III were chosen by the Bureau to provide a range which appears likely to encompass future fertiity.
9. Editors, "The Graying of the Soft-Drink Industry," *Business Week*, May 23, 1977: p. 68.
10. Again the U.S. data are pre-1980 census estimates.
11. The import of this contraction for planning-related analyses cannot be ignored. For example, the traditional intercensus population-estimation procedure used by many small political units is usually premised on a base-level (census count) figure to which additions in succeeding years are a function of net increments of dwelling units multiplied by various average household size multipliers. While shrinking household sizes obviously have direct impact on the shape of the latter, their effect on the base-level population is often ignored. If we conceptualize the base as a fixed stock of dwelling units occupied by households, rather than a total population level per se, then to assume that the population base is fixed in such methodological procedures is dubious. The internal dynamics of the existing stock of dwellings will also reflect household-size changes.
12. In the future, the more general availability of tests of fetal abnormality, which tends to be coupled to elderly primiparas, may make even this prediction hazardous. The dangers involved for both mother and child in elderly childbirth will be much mitigated.
13. Labor force and employment statistics are derived from the Current Population Survey (CPS) undertaken by the Bureau of the Census. The

Bureau of Labor Statistics (U.S. Department of Labor) has the responsibility for analyzing and publishing CPS labor-force data. The following definitions are relevant to the discussion in the text.

Labor Force. The civilian labor force comprises the total of all civilians (noninstitutionalized, 16 years of age and over) classified as employed and unemployed. The total labor force, in addition, includes members of the Armed Forces stationed either in the United States or abroad.

Employment. Employed persons comprise (1) all those who, during the survey week, did any work at all as paid employees, or in their own business, profession, or on their own farm, or who worked 15 hours or more as unpaid workers in a family-operated enterprise, and (2) all those who did not work but had jobs or businesses from which they were temporarily absent due to illness, bad weather, vacation, labor-management dispute, or various personal reasons — whether or not they were seeking other jobs. Each employed person is counted only once.

Unemployment. Unemployed persons include those who did not work at all during the survey week, were looking for work, and were available for work during the reference period except for temporary illness.

Participation Rates represent the proportion of the noninstitution population (16 years of age and over) that is in the labor force (either civilian labor force or total labor force). See U.S. Department of Labor, Bureau of Labor Statistics, *BLS Handbook of Methods for Surveys and Studies*, Bulletin 1910 (Washington, D.C.: Government Printing Office, 1976), pp. 5-7.

14. The savings rate in the United States fell from 8 percent in 1976 to below the 5-percent mark in 1980.
15. The data comprise nonagricultural payroll employment excluding the self-employed and unpaid family workers. The data are published monthly in U.S. Department of Labor, Bureau of Labor Statistics, *Employment and Earnings*.
16. There are eight major employment partitions employed by the Bureau of Labor Statistics. Private nonmanufacturing, as used in Exhibit 39 (and chapter 11), comprise the six nonmanufacturing, nongovernmental sectors: mining, construction, transportation and public utilities, wholesale and retail trade, FIRE (finance, insurance, and real estate), and services.
17. These classifications are similar to those defined in: "America's Restructured Economy," *Business Week* Special Issue, June 1, 1981. Appendix A details their exact composition as derived from the detailed employment sectors published in *Employment and Earnings*.
18. This services sector is broader in composition than that of the Bureau of Labor Statistics (see note 16), which is encompassed in the private nonmanufacturing sector detailed in Exhibit 39.
19. The housing success of the 1970s was facilitated by mortgage instrumentalities — designed for stable, noninflationary economic environments —

extending into a period characterized by strikingly new contours. Fixed-rate mortgages, inadequately reflecting volatile economic conditions, made housing borrowing an unprecedented bargain. The financing of housing in the 1980s will have to meet the challenge of alternative areas of lending and indeed of equity participation. Reindustrialization versus housing may become a confrontation of significant proportions as the nation explicitly considers whether it can afford a pattern of increased housing investment. Implicitly, the demise of long-term, fixed-rate housing finance already serves as an indicator of emerging priorities: the costs of nonessential borrowing must be higher than the rewards. The new instrumentalities — variable-rate and shared-appreciation formats — serve this end, but in turn signal the reduction of housing's unique national priority.

20. Homeownership gains of the 1970s were accomplished in the beginning of the decade by a relatively positive relationship between the costs of acquiring housing and income levels. The end of the decade was characterized by the very fact of inflation increasing housing values — precipitating additional housing demand even at the cost of obvious fiscal stress. The latter marked the maturation of the post-shelter society, a phenomenon unique in its depth to our own time. The long-term chronic inflation of the 1970s altered behavior with equivalent vigor. Housing in America became much more important as a form of investment, as a form of forced savings, and as a refuge from inflation rather than from the elements.
21. This "slowdown" is certainly correlated with surging interest rates and the demise of older housing finance formats.
22. The composition of the regions and divisions are as follows:

NORTHEAST REGION

Middle Atlantic Division	*New England Division*
New York	Maine
New Jersey	New Hampshire
Pennsylvania	Vermont
	Massachusetts
	Rhode Island
	Connecticut

NORTH CENTRAL REGION

East North Central Division

Ohio
Indiana
Illinois
Michigan
Wisconsin

West North Central Division

Minnesota
Iowa
Missouri
North Dakota
South Dakota
Nebraska
Kansas

SOUTH REGION

South Atlantic Division

Delaware
Maryland
District of Columbia
Virginia
West Virginia
North Carolina
South Carolina
Georgia
Florida

East South Central Division

Kentucky
Tennesee
Alabama
Mississippi

West South Central Division

Arkansas
Louisiana
Oklahoma
Texas

WEST REGION

Mountain Division

Montana
Idaho
Wyoming
Colorado
New Mexico
Arizona
Utah
Nevada

Pacific Division

Washington
Oregon
California
Hawaii
Alaska

23. U.S. Bureau of the Census, *Current Population Reports*, Series P-25, no. 640, "Estimates of the Population of States with Components of Change: 1970 to 1975" (Washington, D.C.: U.S. Government Printing Office, November 1976), p. 2.
24. For example, if the Northeast received 1 million overseas immigrants from 1975 to 1979 (hypothetical), and yet had a net outmigration of 700,000 people (actual), then the actual outmigration was 1.7 million people (not considering overseas replacements).
25. The term *agglomeration* is used since metropolitan status in this context includes standard consolidated statistical areas.

Index